triumph over tension

triumph over tension

100 Ways to Relax

By Ruth Winter

GROSSET & DUNLAP
A FILMWAYS COMPANY
Publishers • New York

Contents

1
What Is Tension and Do You Have It?

So you feel tense! Describe that feeling to yourself. Are you "gritting your teeth?" . . . "strung out?" . . . "on edge?" . . . "about to break wide open?" Chances are you have used a phrase that describes a physical condition. We do this all the time. For example, we call people "weak-kneed," "jittery," "stiff necked," "uptight." Yet we often fail to recognize the full extent of the mind's effect on the body and the body's effect on the mind.

In fact, your mind and your body are inseparable! If you doubt this, then just consider for a moment how you react when someone startles you or when the dentist approaches your mouth with his drill: Your heart pounds, your breathing deepens, your muscles tighten—you're tense.

Tension is the body's reaction to threat. It is the physical and mental state which has allowed humans to survive on earth despite many hazards that have caused other species to become extinct.

But tension is not a simple condition. Your job is not tense. Your relationships are not tense. You are tense! And what makes you tense may have no effect whatsoever on another person. Furthermore, you may be tense and not know you are because tension often masquerades as something else; it rarely ever occurs alone.

Tension is usually accompanied by anxiety. Anxiety has been described as "fear spread out thin" or as "a painful uneasiness." Anxiety, like its emotion-mate tension, protects us; it keeps us alert. But when it causes overconcern for the future, when we become apprehensive without just cause, anxiety can become harmful.

How do you know when you are suffering from harmful tension and anxiety? Ask yourself these questions:

	Sometimes	Frequently
• Do you get irritable over petty things?	____	____
• Does your irritability turn into uncontrollable anger?	____	____
• Are you becoming hypercritical of others?	____	____

	Sometimes	Frequently
• Do you feel increasingly sorry for yourself?	——	——
• Are you too busy to eat?	——	——
• Do you have trouble falling asleep?	——	——
• Do you have trouble staying asleep?	——	——
• Are you too tired to think?	——	——
• Are you a nonstop talker?	——	——
• Do you find it difficult to converse?	——	——
• Must you be first in everything?	——	——
• Do minor disappointments throw you?	——	——
• Do you find you have too much to do and too little time to do it in?	——	——
• Are you unable to stop worrying?	——	——
• Are you bored?	——	——
• Do you feel neglected, left out?	——	——
• Do you feel you are indispensable?	——	——
• Do you feel trapped?	——	——
• Do you feel as if you want to run away?	——	——
• Are you anxious about the future?	——	——
• Do your hands tremble?	——	——
• Do you laugh or cry uncontrollably?	——	——
• Do you worry about aches and pains?	——	——
• Are you conscious of the beating of your heart?	——	——
• Do you perspire excessively under the arms?	——	——
• Is your stomach queasy?	——	——
• Do you have pains in your stomach?	——	——
• Do you suffer from dizzy spells?	——	——
• Do you need a tranquilizer or a drink before facing a meeting or a decision?	——	——

Of course any or all of the above symptoms could be due to a physical ailment. And, in fact, you may experience any or all of them during your everyday life. So, answers in the "sometimes" column would merely mean that you are reacting to your environment. But, if you answered "frequently" to any of the questions, you are probably suffering from excess tension.

Just how emotionally distressed or physically sick you become in response to events in your life depends upon your innate personality—your inherited physiology and your life's experiences. But, no matter what causes you to become tense, you *can* learn to counteract this condition and thus become healthier mentally and physically.

In order to really understand tension, and therefore to be able to control it, it's necessary to go back to the beginning of human life on earth. We humans were given a magnificent inborn ability to respond instantly to threat. Upon perceiving danger, our glands secrete powerful chemicals. Sugar is poured into our blood for energy; our red blood cell count goes up to allow prolonged muscle exertion; blood is forced to our heart, lungs, central nervous system, and limbs; our blood pressure rises and our heart beats rapidly, improving circulation for a high rate of oxygen delivery and carbon dioxide pickup. The air sacs in our lungs dilate for better ventilation; our blood's ability to clot is increased in order to prevent blood loss in case of wounding, and, finally, blood is diverted from our abdominal organs, and the regular contractions of our intestinal muscle fibers are inhibited. Our bodies are then ready for a fight or a flight.

For our ancient ancestors in a world of ever-present physical danger, this immediate physiological reaction to threat was absolutely essential; in fact, it enabled them to survive. In addition, their primitive diet and way of life, which forced them to run through the wilderness fleeing from predators or seeking food, kept their bodies in good working order. But today, while there may be some remote physical danger from crime, accidents, and pollution, most of our stresses are emotional. Furthermore, we are a sedentary, easily fed society, so we don't have the release of physical fights or flights to flush the chemical charges from our bodies.

You don't have to be a doctor or a scientist to realize how an unnecessary and often constant chemical and muscular preparation for danger can adversely affect your body. But if it hadn't been for a dangerous honeymoon, we might not know quite as much about the effects of emotions on physical health as we do today. In the early 1900s, Dr. Walter Bradford Cannon, a physiologist, was climbing a mountain when he became precariously wedged in a rock crevice. With enormous effort, he managed to get free, but after the danger was past, he found himself seized by uncontrollable shivers and shakes. While he was shaking, he observed that his apparent anxiety had triggered an autonomic response beyond his conscious ability to control. This so fascinated Dr. Cannon that he began experiments at Harvard which ultimately led to the theory of "fight or flight." Here he theorized that there is a maladaptation to challenge or stress when the state of physiological defense is maintained long beyond the triggering emergency. Fear and rage, he reasoned, cause the blood pressure to rise, and if pent-up emotions are not released, chronic high blood pressure may result. And so the modern science of psychosomatic medicine was born.

Hans Selye, a Canadian physiologist, greatly contributed to psychosomatics with his theories of stress in the 1930s. In his books *The Stress of Life* (McGraw-Hill, 1956) and *Stress Without Distress* (Lippincott, 1974), he points out that the stress syndrome develops in three stages:

1. **Alarm reaction.** This occurs upon sudden exposure to some emotional or physical threat and has two phases: the shock phase, in which the initial and immediate reaction to the threat results in a rise in blood pressure and a quickening of the heartbeat, and the countershock phase, a rebound phenomenon marked by the mobilization of defensive forces. During this latter phase, the adrenal cortex, the outer layers of the gland above the kidney,

is enlarged and there is increased secretion of the powerful adrenocortical hormones.

2. **Resistance stage.** This is marked by full adaptation to the stress during which the symptoms improve or disappear. There is, however, a concurrent decrease in resistance to other stimuli.

3. **Exhaustion stage.** Since adaptability to stress is limited, exhaustion inexorably follows if the stress is sufficiently severe and applied for a prolonged time. Symptoms reappear and, if the stress continues unabated, death ensues.

Fortunately, most physical and emotional stresses fall into the first two categories. But if you have an internal organ which is vulnerable to stress because of heredity or previous injury, that organ will eventually break down, and you could develop a condition such as a bleeding ulcer or a heart attack.

Emotions may kill slowly or quickly. In fact, in certain cultures, witch doctors have been known to cause a superstitious person to drop dead merely by pointing at him or making a suggestion that the victim has been cursed or poisoned. Certainly, laymen have long associated ulcers with repressed anger and stress on the job and tension headaches with aggravation, but now science is pinpointing the chemical basis for such ills. For instance, current studies have shown that tension produces an increase in catecholamine excretion. These catecholamines are chemicals secreted within the body that affect the nervous system.

Tension has also been shown to increase the fats, triglycerides, and cholesterol in the blood. High levels of these have been associated with hardening of the arteries, heart attacks, and strokes. On the other hand, the body's chemical reactions which have nothing to do with outside events may cause you to become emotionally tense. The obvious examples are premenstrual tension, postpartum depression, and menopause. But schizophrenia, manic-depressive illness, and some other emotional maladies are also thought to be innately chemical rather than outwardly environmental.

In 1967 doctors clearly demonstrated for the first time that anxiety attacks could be predictably produced in humans by a specific chemical stimulus. It was discovered that people suffering from anxiety neurosis produce more lactate when they exercise than other people. Lactate is the salt of lactic acid which is manufactured when muscles are exercised. When scientists injected lactate into neurotics and into controls, both groups became anxious; but the neurotics had a more severe reaction than the other participants. When calcium was given first and then lactate, the anxiety symptoms were prevented. Why? No one as yet understands.

There is no doubt that our ability to tolerate stress is genetically based. Right from the moment of birth, some infants react more strongly than others to stimuli such as light and noise. And there are some scientists who believe that our emotions can be affected even before birth. In animal work at Villanova University, for instance, Dr. Ingebord Ward found that mothers who underwent stress during pregnancy produced sons with more feminine traits, biological and behavioral, than mothers who did not. Dr. Robert M. Rose of Boston University School of Medicine determined that soldiers under stress of combat training usually had lower testosterone, the male hormone, in their blood, than soldiers at officers candidate school. It has also been reported that investigators are able to determine which monkey will be king of the pack just by measuring the levels of testosterone in their urine.

However, even though there are genetic, inborn factors of stress toleration, there is no doubt that the way we, as children, are raised is also important. Youngsters raised in homes where there is an atmosphere of calm, assurance, and stability will tend to reflect these charac-

teristics themselves and to be relatively free of anxiety
and tension later on in life. On the other hand, children
brought up in an atmosphere of uncertainty, worry, and
anxiety will tend to grow up worrisome, insecure, and
anxious.

Young people, in fact, suffer from tension just as
adults do, but their symptoms may be somewhat different. Stress disorders in childhood may manifest themselves as lack of appetite, temper tantrums, constipation,
coughing, headbanging, head rolling, pica, breath holding, thumb sucking, nail biting, body rocking, excessive
masturbation, tics, bed wetting, soiling, stammering, and
fidgeting. Indeed, chronic nervous activity, sometimes
included in the category of "hyperactivity," is often a
sign that a child is under tension. His anger may be
aroused. He may have been refused some satisfaction
which he feels necessary, and he becomes tense when he
is not permitted to express that anger.

Parents can usually recognize the symptoms; but the
child's tension makes them tense themselves. Mothers
and fathers may attempt to teach a youngster self-control
too early. This makes matters worse. The anger the child
feels which is repressed may then show itself as whim-
pering or an eye tic, both of which are actually dry
crying. By allowing a child the freedom to cry, tears become emotional first aid, and the youngster is then better able to face the next frustration.

Tension, for both adults and children, is a normal part
of our everyday activity. Without it we would find life
dull and our productivity low. But there is a difference
between beneficial tension and harmful pressure. Indeed, tension can cause or contribute to ill health ranging from a mild emotional upset to severe physical and
mental impairment and even death. (See Life Events
Stress Quiz, page 81.)

We are all like bridges; some of us, because of our
physiological makeup and our upbringing, can take a

heavier load of stress. Others find life a series of big and little tensions; and minor problems, which most people ignore, throw these people into emotional and physical chaos. Each of us has our own stress point. If we go over that point, we are anxious and unhappy, and, in the end, inefficient. If we go too far over, we break. If we are below our stress point, we do not achieve our true potential and the satisfaction of accomplishment. If we go too far under, we vegetate.

You can, and certainly should, learn the point at which pressure creates harmful tension in yourself. You can, and certainly should, learn to prevent harmful tension and to counteract it should it occur.

Tension remains, grows, and corrodes when it is bottled up. It goes away when you remove the cork by taking action. This book intends to demonstrate the many proven scientific methods of releasing tension.

2
Drugs to Ease Tension

Can drugs ease your feelings of tension? Some can, easily. But at what price?

When psychopharmaceuticals were introduced in this country in 1954 to combat mental illness, some argued that they were curealls for the emotional ills of man and that they were ushering in a new era of tranquility. Others maintained they were morally bad; they would arrest human development and could, therefore, be used for social control.

But during the little more than two decades that these drugs have been in use, there is little doubt that psychopharmaceuticals have made a tremendous impact on our society. Just two years after they were introduced, the number of patients in psychiatric hospitals—for the first time in 175 years—began to decline. And some of these discharged patients had been in residence for more than twenty years. It is estimated that this emptying out of our mental hospitals has saved us more than six billion dollars.

On the other hand, we have been spending about a billion dollars a year on psychopharmaceuticals. The prescription rate for them increased 42 percent between 1964 and 1970. In 1974, 13 percent of all adult men and 29 percent of all adult women have used or are using prescribed psychoactive drugs.

The use of illegal drugs such as marijuana, heroin, amphetamines, LSD, and cocaine can only be estimated, but these also are termed psychopharmaceuticals, since they are used to alter mood and to relieve emotional tension.

Alcohol is still another psychopharmaceutical. It is not a tranquilizer; it is a euphoriant. But drinking may not necessarily produce a release from tension; in fact, it usually reinforces the prevailing mood. So if you are tranquil, you will become more tranquil; if you are tense and irritable, you will become more tense and irritable.

The introduction of tranquilizers in the form of prescribed medication has vastly altered our concept of mental illness. It has allowed us to increasingly accept a physiological, rather than a social, cause of emotional disorders, thus reducing some of the stigma associated with them. It is generally agreed today that every psychoactive drug works by affecting the biochemical abnormalities responsible for the symptoms. For instance, it is known that nonreproductive hormones may effect aggressive behavior in humans. When the adrenal glands above the kidneys secrete too much adrenalin, the substance that helps prepare us for flight or fight, we become tense and quick to anger. The same holds true for the secretions of the thyroid gland in the neck. Those who have too much of its hormone are highly excitable, tense, and have a strong tendency to respond angrily to frustrating circumstances. And when adrenalin and thyroid hormone levels are reduced in the blood, we become more relaxed.

The sex hormones, the female estrogen and the male testosterone, are known to affect behavior. Women who are depressed have high levels of monamine oxidase (MAO) in the blood. MAO is a brain enzyme which interferes with the transmission of messages sent between the nerve cells in the brain. In normal women, the MAO blood count is 500 to 1000 per minute. In depressed women, however, it ranges from 20,000 to 30,000. When these women are given high doses of estrogen, the MAO count is greatly reduced and so is their depression because estrogen is a MAO inhibitor.

Estrogen can be considered a psychopharmaceutical, for like other drugs in this category, it acts on those brain chemicals which transmit electrical signals between the nerve cells in the brain. Among such chemicals already identified by scientists are dopamine, norepinephrine, and serotonin. These are manufactured from substances circulating in the blood plasma and are stored in nerve cells to await a triggering signal. When triggered, they send an electrochemical message to a neighboring cell which, in turn, shoots electrical impulses down the receiving nerve. During depression, these electrical transmissions are believed to be too weak, while during anxiety, tension, and some psychosis, the transmissions are too rapid—too irregular. When we are depressed, our nerves can't hear each other's signals; when we are tense and anxious, there are so many rapid signals that the transmissions become confused.

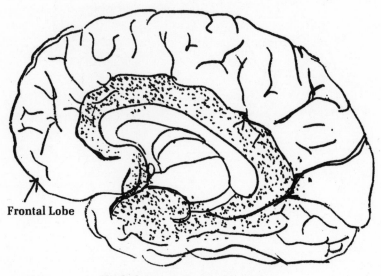

Frontal Lobe

Shaded Area Is the Limbic System

Psychoactive pharmaceuticals work on the cells in a specific area of the brain called the "limbic system." This is so named because its structures—including the amygdala and the thalamus—rim the brain and are in a sort of "limbo." The limbic system is our emotional switchboard; everytime we feel an emotion, the electrical activity within this system changes. In fact, various types of aggression may be caused or haulted by destruction or stimulation of the amygdala within the limbic switchboard. Anatomists have been able to pinpoint from nine to fourteen different anatomical amygdala areas which can produce changes in behavior ranging from terrifying rage to unshakable placidity.

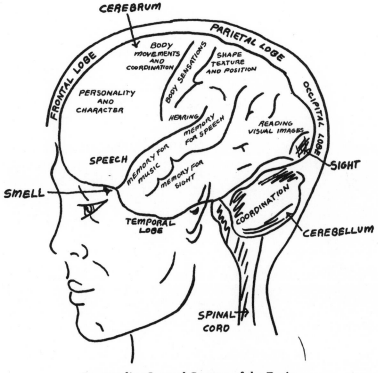

Personality Control Centers of the Brain

Human tension and anxiety have also been produced by stimulation of the hypothalamus within the limbic system, but these emotions have been permanently relieved by electrocoagulation of that part of the brain.

There are three main categories of prescribed drugs which affect the signals within the limbic switchboard. These include major tranquilizers, minor tranquilizers and antidepressants.

Major tranquilizers

Psychosis is the most severe form of mental illness. Its symptoms include altered personality, inability to distinguish between what is real and what is imagined, deep depression, and bizarre thoughts, including delusions and hallucinations. Schizophrenia, in its various forms, is the most common psychosis.

The major tranquilizers, such as Thorazine or Mellaril, act on the limbic system. Their action is tied in with the brain chemical serotonin, and it takes them about two weeks to reach their optimum effect. It is known that when drugs are given which alter the brain serotonin content, mental aberrations occur. Those drugs which act like serotonin, such as LSD, cause mental excitement and hallucinations. The tranquilizing drugs subdue schizophrenic agitation by causing a reduction of serotonin in the brain and other tissues. On the other hand, a deficiency of serotonin is believed to cause mental depression.

Ironically, tranquilization is not a prominent feature of the major tranquilizers. The drugs may reduce overactivity and belligerent behavior, but they do so by affecting the underlying brain pathology. Sedation occurs only in the early stages of the drug therapy in certain susceptible individuals and usually when the drugs are used in excessive doses. Proof that tranquilizers affect underlying pathology is that 70 percent of the acute schizophrenics who receive no drug therapy after release from the hospital are readmitted within one year, while only 20 to 30 percent of those receiving tranquilizers at home are readmitted.

But tranquilizers are powerful chemicals and they do have serious side effects, some of which show up only after long periods of time. For instance, an estimated 5 percent of the patients exposed to long-term therapy with such drugs develop a condition called tardive dyskinesia. This is characterized by smacking of the lips, protrusion of the tongue, and blowing of the cheeks, as well as side-to-side movements and other bizarre muscular abnormalities. It is similar in symptoms to Huntington's disease, a hereditary degenerative brain condition which occurs in young adulthood. Major tranquilizers can also cause permanent skin and eye changes and, in rare cases, sudden death from what is believed to be an irregularity of the heart rhythm. Indeed, major tranquilizers are useful drugs but they are certainly not to be taken lightly.

Minor tranquilizers

Neurosis covers a wide variety of mental ailments, ranging from minor maladjustments to handicapping phobias. Here the most common symptoms are anxiety and tension. In the past, neurotics were told to "Go home and get a hold of yourself!"

Neurosis is less severe than other mental ills but is believed to have a biological, as well as environmental, base. It involves thoughts, feelings, and actions which persist despite their inappropriateness, and is due to a reverberation of nerve impulses within that seat of emotions, the brain's limbic system. These reverberations— or electric impulses—keep shooting through the brain's nerve cells. Tranquilizers, theoretically, slow down such reverberations. In fact, when a tranquilizer is given before electric shock treatments, used to combat depression, the electrical effect is muted.

Among the most widely used minor tranquilizers are Librium, Valium, and Miltown. These are prescribed to relieve mild to severe tension. Addiction to them is rare but withdrawal symptoms have been noted in some cases. The tranquilizers may cause drowsiness, confusion, loss of balance, and skin pigmentation, as well as allergic reactions, so they, also, are not to be taken lightly.

Antidepressants

Everyone gets depressed sometime or other, and this depression is often concomitant with tension. But there are severe, incapacitating, lasting depressions which require intensive medical therapy.

Chronic depression often masquerades as tension and anxiety, phobia, obsession, hypothyroidism, diabetes, chronic prostatitis, colitis, or a variety of other ills. According to the National Institute of Mental Health, in any given year 15 percent of adults between the ages of eighteen and seventy-four years suffer significant depressive symptoms; 23 percent of admissions to mental hospitals and 30 percent of admissions to psychiatric units of general hospitals are for depression.

There are basically two types of depression, unipolar and bipolar. The bipolar depressions are those in which the victim alternates between manic highs and deep depressions, usually regardless of circumstances. The unipolar depressions are more subject to environmental influences and may occur in the mother after childbirth, for instance, or with the loss of a job or a mate. In addition, there is another type of depression associated with psychosis, but this is usually listed under schizophrenia, because it carries with it hallucinations and delusions.

In the mid-1950s, it was discovered that chemicals which interfere with the release of the enzyme monamine oxidase, mentioned earlier in this chapter, could lift depressions. It is theorized that MAO plays a part in the breakdown of certain brain chemicals, particularly serotonin, epinephrine, and norepinephrine, and causes a deficiency in them which leads to depression. But MAO inhibitors have serious side effects, particularly if they are combined with foods high in the chemical tyramine, such as wine, herring, or cheese. The combination causes the blood pressure to shoot up dangerously.

In 1959, a new class of drugs, the tricyclics, were introduced for depression. Although related to the tranquilizers, they increase rather than decrease the brain chemical norepinephrine. The tricyclics take at least twenty-one days to become effective, and they must be given in sufficient doses to combat depression. However, in some cases, MAO inhibitors work better than the tricyclics, which do not have as many side effects and are considered safer.

For the bipolar, or manic–depressive, illness, the drug lithium entered the marketplace in the late 1960s. It is very effective in actually preventing the highs and lows of the disease from occurring. Joshua Logan, the Broadway producer, has proclaimed its benefits widely and said that he has had no signs of his chronic illness since taking the medication.

Various antidepressant medications have helped thousands who suffer from "the loss of pleasure." But these drugs are not universally effective. They are also not used as widely as they might be. In the past two decades that they have been on the market, they have been unable to slow down the suicide rate which has climbed to 30,000 Americans a year. Suicide is the end product of unbearable tension.

When does normal tension turn into stress so severe that a person takes his or her life to relieve the discomfort? The answer to that question is usually found only after the fact. But one thing is certain: If tension is caught at the beginning, treated, and relieved, self-destruction can be prevented. Emergencies are always more difficult to treat.

Are over-the-counter, nonprescription drugs the answer? Such medications are sold for the advertised purpose of inducing sleep or relieving daily tensions. The ingredients most commonly used in such preparations are methapyrilene, scopolamine, various bromides, aspirin, and salicylamide. Methapyrilene is an antihistamine which may help your allergies and cause you to be sleepy, but won't relieve your tension—that is, unless you think it will. It is the weakest of the antihistamines. Scopolamine a mild sedative derived from belladonna cannot promote or maintain sleep, and it can be toxic.

Bromides, which can accumulate in the body, may cause delirium, heart problems, and hallucinations.

No drug, prescription or nonprescription, which affects your mind should be taken without medical supervision. On the other hand, drugs which reduce tension and produce a more calm and relaxed mood can be very useful. It is not a sign of weakness to employ them when necessary any more than it is a sign of weakness to use a jack to aid your muscles when changing a tire.

Not all people respond to tranquilizers in the same way. Neither do animals. For instance, in a study done with wolves, it was found that when the animals were given tranquilizers the adult wolves could be socialized within days rather than months. However, when the drugs were withdrawn, the socialized behavior dropped away, and the animals reverted to their untamed behavior. In other words, tranquilizers helped the wolves overcome fear and aggression, but only during the period the drugs were given. The learning did not carry over to the undrugged state. On the other hand, with dogs, a close relative of the wolf, the story was different. Tranquilizers were given to dogs raised in isolation and therefore extremely frightened of man. The dogs' fears were calmed by the tranquilizers, and they were quickly domesticated. Unlike the wolf, when the medicine was stopped the dogs did not regress—they remained friendly. This led researchers at the University of Chicago to conclude that early-life experiences do indeed affect behavior, but that genetics also play an important role. Therefore, tranquilization with drugs is dependent, in part, upon heredity.

There is still much to be learned about all psychopharmaceuticals. The drugs have been used for great good, but they have also been proved harmful. The Russians allegedly administer powerful tranquilizers— which dull the mind—to politically disaffected intellectuals. Tranquilizers are sometimes used in this country to keep elderly nursing home patients, mental institution inmates, and young children quieter and less troublesome instead of hiring sufficient personnel to deal directly with their underlying problems.

Dr. Frank Ayd of Baltimore, a nationally known psychiatrist, discussing the impact of biological psychiatry, once observed: "It is clear that chemicals affect the functioning of the brain and that we are now able to influence the brain in ways heretofore impossible. As the chemistry of the brain is more definitely known and a growing range of drugs that affect its function are synthesized, an increasingly extensive and precise influence over how a person thinks, feels, and behaves surely will be possible."

He concluded, "Whether we shall be praised or cursed by our children's children will depend on how much we succeed today in being aware of the value of human life and of our extensive obligation to the individual and to all of society."

We humans are apparently the only animals that know we will die. Thus anxiety and tension can never be entirely relieved unless we pay the price of dulling our intellectual functions.

Some tension is useful and necessary. Drugs can reduce tension. They can literally be lifesavers. But drugs are certainly not the whole answer. There are other ways to deal with tension.

3
Your Mind
over Your
Matter

You can overcome tension and achieve relaxation using the power of your mind alone. There are, in this chapter, descriptions of the latest and the most ancient methods of mind over matter control. And these involve no magic, nor do they require special skills; indeed, almost anyone can employ them.

If you don't believe you control your mind, if you say to yourself you have no *willpower*, then try this easy experiment. Walk over to the window and inhale deeply and rapidly twenty times. Do you feel dizzy? You should! You have deliberately lowered the carbon dioxide in your blood. When people overbreathe during nervous tension, it's called "hyperventilation." Doctors often recommend that hyperventilators breathe into a brown paper bag during nervous attacks to build up the carbon dioxide in their blood.

The various methods of inducing relaxation, including biofeedback, Transcendental Meditation, rational emotive therapy, hypnosis, Silva mind control and progressive relaxation, all have two things in common—suggestibility and self-control. Biofeedback, for instance, allows a person to manipulate body processes previously assumed uncontrollable by observing visible records of their workings. Transcendental Meditation, born in India, is a state of learned relaxation. Hypnosis involves tenacious concentration.

Dr. Ernest Hilgard of the department of psychology at Stanford University, whose field is hypnosis research, explains that with Transcendental Meditation, biofeedback, or hypnosis, you can alter your hand temperature and cause one of your hands to become warmer than the other. "The locus of control may be different. You may feed your body different signals but the result is the same."

All the techniques in this chapter have their loyal advocates. But the methods work, and the one that is best is the one that works for you!

Biofeedback

Once upon a time, scientists believed that there were two types of muscle control in your body, voluntary and involuntary. With the voluntary muscles you could raise your hand, turn your head, lift your foot. With the involuntary muscles you had no control over the smooth muscles working your internal organs. Your heartbeat, digestion, and blood-vessel contractions were all beyond your ability to regulate.

Then developments in the field of electronics made it possible for us to actually visualize various internal signals such as muscle tension, blood pressure, and skin temperature—even brain waves. The heart's electrical activity is measured by the electrocardiograph; the brain's by the electroencephalograph, and the muscles' by the electromyograph. The skin's response is measured with a dermohmeter.

The lie detector, which has been used for more than a decade, determines truthfulness by measuring the heart and breathing rate and the skin's response to a question asked. A lie is a psychological emergency and causes the body to react physiologically to the resulting stress.

Only recently have these machines which measure such body signals been able to convert them into recognizable signals to inform the subject of what is going on. An integrated system exists which gives the information back to you about how you are functioning. A light, a bell, a tone, or a graph may be used.

You, of course, have always watched signals. Observing signals and reacting to them is the way you learned such skills as driving a car or playing baseball. But you used your voluntary muscle system to do it. For instance, when you see a red light, you take your foot off the gas and put it on the brake. The stop light is the signal. The motion of your foot is the biofeedback.

But it was not recognized until just a few years ago that

you could do the same thing with your involuntary muscle system. For some reason not yet completely understood, when you can see what is happening to your heart or brain, you can learn to control its functioning to an amazing degree. The ability to learn such control is inherent in you and every rational human being.

Dr. Neal Miller of Rockefeller University, New York City, and Dr. Elmer Green and his wife, Alyce, of the Menninger Foundation in Kansas, have been pioneers in the field of biofeedback. Dr. Miller has been able to teach rabbits to blush in only one ear and humans to reduce their blood pressure with just their minds.

It is true that blood pressure can be lowered momentarily by merely breathing deeply. It can also be raised by tightening the skeletal muscles. So, to rule out these two factors, Dr. Miller experimented with paralyzed patients in artificial lungs who could not control their own respiration and with muscular dystrophy victims who could not tense their muscles. He found that both groups could alter their blood pressure at will after learning the techniques. In the past, Dr. Miller observes, researchers were convinced that the responses of the glands and viscera were primitive and not susceptible to direct control as are our fingers and hands. "We now know that the viscera are represented in the highest level of the brain—the cortex; perhaps not to the same degree as the fingers or lips, but they are in the cortex."

He points out that visceral learning—or biofeedback —is similar to all learning. It is by trial and error. We are taught in basic training when we are young to control our skeletal muscles. If we did not learn to use them early, we could not fight or flee, and mankind would have become extinct. But we do not train our children to consciously perceive what is happening inside their bodies; we make them learn subconsciously.

For instance, he continues, a child who does not want to go to school because he is not prepared for an exam-

ination may have a variety of physical symptoms,
a queasy stomach at one time and pallor and faintn
another. At this point, his mother, who is particul
concerned about the cardiovascular symptoms of pall
and faintness, says: "You are sick, you must stay home."
She frees him from fear, and his reward reinforces his
cardiovascular response to stress. On the other hand, a
mother who concentrates on the gastrointestinal symp-
toms in her child's reaction to stress will reinforce his
gastrointestinal response. In other words, this might very
well be why some people have bad hearts when exposed
to stress and some have ulcers.

Menninger's Dr. Elmer and Alyce Green have studied
those with the greatest known control over their bod-
ies—yogis. For instance, the Greens hooked up a forty-
five-year-old swami, Rama, to a biofeedback apparatus.
Rama was trained in the Himalayas and showed the
Greens how he could make the temperature of the little
finger side of his right palm different from the tempera-
ture of the thumb side by 10 degrees F. He did this feat
apparently by controlling the flow of blood in the large
arteries of the wrist without moving or using muscle ten-
sion. He just turned the blood flow on and off. Rama also
demonstrated to the Greens that he could stop his heart
from pumping blood and could produce specific brain-
wave patterns on demand.

The Greens said Rama explained his physiological
feats by saying: "All of the body is in the mind but not all
of the mind is in the body." Dr. Elmer Green said, "In yo-
gic theory, the mind is not merely a person's perception
of involuntary electrochemical changes in the body. On
the contrary, the body is only the densest section of an
energy field that includes both the mind and body. It is
interesting to remember that our bodies, like everything
else in the universe, are electromagnetic fields with
swarms of particles as dense portions. We are almost en-
tirely empty space, although we see ourselves and all na-

ture as solid matter because that is the way we were con-
structed by evolution to see."

Now the swami's ability took years and years of training and involves a way of life and philosophy quite different from ours. But with American ingenuity, the prin-
ciples of yogic control over the body have been adapted
to electronic technology. You *can* learn to control your
inner workings, and therefore you can learn to relax
and reduce tension. It is really quite simple. As pointed
out before, when muscles tense they fire out electrical
impulses which can be recorded and transformed into
some sort of tone, light or graph so you can tell immediately whether you are tensing or relaxing your muscles.

If you have tension headaches—the most common type
of headache—the electrodes are put on your forehead.
When you tighten the muscles of your brow, an electrical
impulse is emitted. The more tense the muscles become,
the louder the signal, because the tenser the muscles, the
greater the amount of electricity they emit. You can
transfer the current into a tone or a series of clicks, so
that the more "uptight" you get, the higher the tone or
the faster the clicks. You then attempt to relax your muscles. You don't furrow your brow or squeeze your eyelids together. You imagine your forehead being smooth
and relaxed. You think of yourself in a peaceful place,
such as on a lake or in a lounge chair in the warm sun.

The skill of relaxing your forehead muscles is learned,
just as you learn tennis or golf. Once you begin to know
how it feels to relax, you can relax on cue. You can actually learn how to have relaxed brain waves. In fact,
control of brain waves can be mastered so skillfully that
epileptics can be taught to prevent seizures.

Alpha waves, which equal eight to twelve cycles per
second, are associated with a pleasant, relaxed state
without any type of imagery. If you start thinking or
forming images, the rhythms are broken up and get much
faster. Alpha rhythm may be related to meditation. All

you have to do is close your eyes, relax, and not think of anything, and you will probably go into alpha.

Using a thermometer to measure temperature in the extremities is still another form of biofeedback. Learning to increase the temperature in the hands and thus increase the blood flow is an exercise from autogenic training, a voluntary control system begun by a German physician, Dr. Johannes Schultz, in 1910. He found that learning to control muscle tension and body warmth encouraged recovery from many psychosomatic diseases.

You have to relax your involuntary muscle system in order to warm the hand. Once learned, the ability to warm your hand through biofeedback seems to alleviate dysfunctions in other blood vessel areas. In the same way, people who suffer from migraine headaches, which are vascular, are helped when they learn to warm their hands.

Biofeedback training for self-regulation of blood flow has also been shown to help many patients suffering from Raynaud's disease (a deficiency in circulation to the extremities), tension headaches, and heart disease.

A simpler technique which does not require training is of help to people who grind their teeth. An electrode is attached to the jaw muscle, and whenever the jaw muscles tense, a tone goes off in a small ear device.

Another quite successful use of biofeedback involves insomnia. Some people cannot relax enough to allow sleep to envelope them. By using electrodes attached to their forehead muscles, a tone is sounded. The more tense they are, the louder the tone. The more they relax, the softer the sound. However, it does not always work. Some insomniacs are able to lower the tone right down to zero but they still cannot fall asleep.

Biofeedback, because it teaches self-mastery, has been successfully used to treat some alcoholics and some drug addicts. However, this is certainly not the answer to everything for everyone. There is no doubt that if your muscles are relaxed, you are more likely to feel relaxed. There is evidence that feedback helps with moment-to-moment tension stages but has little effect on how you are chronically or habitually. It can't change what is making you tense.

Furthermore, treatment may sensitize you to your tension. It may make you more aware that you are tense and therefore make you more tense when you try to control it.

Do not go out and buy a commercial biofeedback machine (there are several varieties on the market). If you want to pursue this technique, you need to work with a qualified psychologist or psychiatrist.

Hypnosis

Hypnosis has been romanticized. Indeed, some hypnotists are reputed to have supernatural powers and great control over your behavior. The truth is that hypnosis is merely suggestion, and if anyone has any power over you, it is you. As far back as 150 years ago, Abbé Faria recognized that the responsibility for entering into the hypnotic state rests more on the subject's ability than on the hypnotist's skill. This is not to say, however, that hypnosis should be taken lightly. It is an intrusive measure and should not be used as a parlor game. In fact, one man who learned to hypnotize himself inadvertently went into a trance while driving and careened off the highway.

Some people can be hypnotized and some cannot. The difference is in suggestibility and in defenses. In 1959 Dr. M. T. Orne reported in the *Journal of Abnormal and Social Psychiatry* a little experiment he performed with a group of hypnotized males. He instructed them to hold a 1-kilogram weight at arm's length with the suggestion that they hallucinate a table supporting the extended arm and to feel no pain or fatigue. These subjects were able to keep their arms extended for an average of about five-and-one-half minutes, certainly an outstanding feat. But these same men, when subsequently strongly urged in a nonhypnotized state to surpass their previous performance under hypnosis, maintained their arms extended for an average of seven minutes. Orne noted that it is possible that if they had received the same degree of urging under hypnosis they might have done even better. His aim was merely to demonstrate that a remarkable feat performed under hypnosis could also be performed by other means.

Dr. Paul Wachtel of the Research Center for Mental Health at New York University points out that clinical reports of dramatic alterations of experience and psychophysiological functioning under hypnosis continue to appear regularly in the scientific literature. But just as often there are reports of experimental studies which question the genuineness of hypnotic phenomena. Dr. Wachtel said it may be that the experimenter's bias may cause both the negative and the positive findings.

But whether it is called hypnosis, meditation, or some other state, autosuggestion can be an effective way to relax. Self-hypnosis is synonomous with self-discipline and motivation. Suggestion is the key.

You can suggest to yourself that you want to relax. Here's how to do it:

Go into a quiet room and lie down. Remove your shoes, open your collar, belt, or any other restricting clothing. Close your eyes. Take five slow, deep breaths. Say to yourself that you are going to relax all your muscles. You can employ the frequently used progressive relaxation techniques. Start with your toes. Tense them and then relax them. Then tense both your feet and relax them. Tense your calf muscles and relax them. Progress from muscle group to muscle group until you reach your forehead muscles. Always tense and then relax.

While tensing and relaxing your muscles, tell yourself

that you are relaxing . . . letting go . . . floating away from tension, anger, fear, all unpleasant thoughts. Tell yourself that your eyelids are so heavy you can't hold them open. Tell yourself that the bed or couch is holding you up because you are such a relaxed body. You should achieve total relaxation. The more you use the technique, the easier it will be.

There is another similar way to hypnotize yourself. Sit in a chair and look at a spot on the wall. Tell yourself that your eyelids are heavy, very heavy—so heavy you can't keep them open. Close your eyes slowly. Take five deep breaths. Let your shoulders relax . . . your abdomen relax . . . your knees relax so they are apart. Tell yourself that your right arm is heavy, very heavy—so heavy that you can't hold it up. Keep concentrating on your right arm until you feel it is heavy. Then open your eyes and stretch. If you keep practicing this technique, eventually you will be able to just concentrate on your right arm and by association feel relaxed immediately. And you wil be able to perform this autosuggestion relaxation anywhere, and at anytime.

Transcendental Meditation

There is a burgeoning following for the teachings of Maharishi Mahesh Yogi, who first came to public view when Mia Farrow and the Beatles sought peace at his feet in India. Transcendental Meditation (TM), which he advocates, is now being taught by hundreds of teachers from the International Meditation Society.

The meditator usually goes into a quiet environment and sits in a comfortable position. He or she must try to shut out other stimuli and repeat a personal, secret word called a "mantra." The repetition frees the meditator from logical, externally oriented thought. The eyes must remain closed throughout the "quiet time." This is supposed to be done for twenty minutes twice a day, usually before breakfast and before dinner.

There is no doubt that TM is beneficial to many people. Studies done at Harvard and at the University of California have shown that during meditation oxygen consumption and metabolic rate markedly decrease, indicating a state of deep rest. Brain patterns are within the 8- to 9-cycle-per-second range, indicating a state of restful alertness.

Meditators have been found to have improved memory and learning ability, and to have increased emotional stability. One woman I interviewed said that Transcendental Meditation helped her get through a divorce and a broken leg which happened soon afterward. It also helped her children to adjust to their parents' breakup. Another woman, who was a confirmed cynic about meditation before the tragedy of losing a child drove her to the edge of suicide, told me that Transcendental Meditation enabled her to survive.

TM has both physiological and emotional benefits, but it is somewhat cultish, and thus dissuades people from trying it. In fact, as we have seen here, the same benefits can be achieved without the ceremony.

Silva mind control

This organization was begun by a Mexican-American, Jose Silva, in 1966. The Silva mind control course takes forty-eight hours—usually four consecutive, twelve-hour days. It involves entering a series of mental states to achieve Alpha, the mental state one enters when one is alert but relaxed. At this point, the brain waves, or alpha waves as they are called, occur at the rate of ten per second. When concentration begins, however, these alpha waves disappear, and the brain wave recordings indicate faster, smaller waves known as beta waves.

Just as in TM, you have to select a quiet spot, a comfortable position, and you have to try to shut out extraneous stimuli. Close your eyes. Deeply relax your muscles by progressive relaxation (see pages 31–32), if necessary.

Breathe through your nose and be aware of your breathing. As you breathe out, you say a word associated with peace and calmness such as "sea" or "love" or "sky." Say the word silently to yourself each time you breathe out. Continue for twenty minutes. Periodically open your eyes and check the time. When you finish, sit quietly for several minutes, at first with your eyes closed and then later with them open. If you are not successful in achieving a deep level of relaxation, don't worry. By practice, you will, if you keep trying, be able to achieve it.

Use your imagination

Rational Emotive Therapy or Rational Behavior Training is based on the acceptance of objective reality: "Telling it like it is." It enables you to achieve a self-determined goal, and creates a minimum of significant internal conflict with your environment.

Dr. Maxie C. Maultsby Jr., director of the outpatient psychiatric department, University of Kentucky School of Medicine, uses this technique for treating patients. The author of *Emotional Well-Being Through Rational Behavior Training*, with David S. Goodman, Dr. Maultsby says that RBT teaches people to increase their reasoning skills so they'll be better able to deal with problems and stresses in daily living. The method is based on the fact that the ability to think logically enables one to keep his emotions under better control, to see problems more clearly, and to solve them more effectively.

Dr. Maultsby advises a subject to write down the facts of the event that occurred at the time of the emotional upset. He is to state only the concise, as-it-happened facts. Then, in the next column, he is to write down the feelings he had at the time of the event. Was he angry? Sad? Embarrassed? In a third column, he is to write down why he thinks he felt that way. The psychiatrists urge the person to be objective and rational.

The next step in the process after the event has been pinpointed and the reaction and reason for it have been stated, is for the subject to imagine himself again in the situation. Then he thinks about behaving in a way he would have liked to behave and the rational reason he should behave that new way.

Another form of this therapy involves deliberately thinking about the situation that made you tense. Consciously observe the effects of that tension—rapid breathing, tight muscles, distress. Write down or say out loud how you feel. Then try one of the various relaxation techniques mentioned previously.

If you find you cannot relax, repeat the mental image of what made you tense and again concentrate on the symptoms of your tension—the tight muscles, the rapid breathing, perhaps the headache—then relax again. Keep repeating until you are over the upset.

Still another technique, one which is the easiest of all the imagery ones, involves lying in your bed just before you go to sleep, and reviewing the events of the day starting with the last ones first. While recalling the descending order of things, when you come to something that made you tense, stop and revise the scene. Make the event happen in your mind as you would have wanted it to occur. Then go on to the next. By doing this, you can defuse the situations that play over and over again in your mind and make you tense.

Behavior modification.

Behavior modification is relatively new; only in the past thirty years have experimentally derived, scientific concepts been used to change behavior patterns in a systematic fashion. The behavioral approach is affected by the environmental events which precede or follow it. In treatment, for instance, a thorough understanding of the present conditions which make you tense would be sought, rather than what it was in your past that caused you to react that way.

Dr. John Paul Brady of the University of Pennsylvania, one of the foremost practitioners of behavior modification, uses a tiny electronic metronome to help patients combat tension. The metronome, which he developed and which is designed to be worn in the ear, is very effective. His patients learn to relax and unwind to the rhythmic cadence of its beating. After an initial session, the mini-metronome can be used at home, in the office—or wherever tension occurs.

Metronome-conditioned relaxation (MCR) is aimed at releasing that muscular tightness. At first, the patient is instructed to tighten and then relax eight major muscle groups—again, progressive relaxation (see pages 31–32). Next the patient listens to a twenty-five-minute taped recording of Dr. Brady instructing in a melodious voice, "re—lax and let go." A metronome is set at about sixty beats per minute and it strikes gently in the background. Gradually, the voice fades, and only the ticking of the metronome remains.

"The idea is to build up an association between the beats of the metronome and relaxation," Dr. Brady says. "In time, the metronome will function as conditioned stimuli and therefore, automatically elicit relaxation."

He says it usually takes about five to ten MCR lessons before the patient is reliably able to attain a deeply relaxed state. But "once trained, the patient can listen to the tapes or the tiny metronome whenever he feels tension mounting or a headache coming on. What it means is that the patient is able to carry his therapy with him wherever he goes."

There are many other behavior therapy techniques being used around the country. No matter which method you choose, make yourself proficient, so you will be able to find peace.

4
Tension
at Work

Work is important to your mental health, for when your skills and abilities are used to their fullest, your emotional and material needs can be satisfied. Work can reassure you of your self-worth, keep you in touch with life, and give you a sense of achievement, well-being, and personal growth.

Today's work, however, is rarely a pleasure, whether it is in an office, at home, or outdoors. In fact, according to many social scientists, work is the most common cause of tension. It is only the rare person in our society who, like the village blacksmith of Henry Wadsworth Longfellow's poem, can say his ". . . brow is wet with honest sweat/He earns what'er he can,/And looks the whole world in the face,/For he owes not any man."

We owe—boy, do we owe! We have a compulsion to obtain new things. We believe the more we have, the happier we'll be. As a result, many of us measure ourselves by what we have, rather than by what we are.

Dr. A. Moneim El-Meligi, an Egyptian-born professor of organizational psychology at Rutgers Graduate School of Business Administration, Newark, New Jersey, says that because of our compulsion to obtain new things, it is hard to find an organization that is producing solely what it set out to produce. "You have to keep producing new things. New materials are being discovered that might outdate older ones. You must keep abreast of the times. So you create a vicious cycle. Not only are you highly competitive with others but with yourself."

He adds that we all feel we have to keep plugging to retain our position; mobility is so great that there seems to be constant danger of falling down the ladder. In other countries, the Rutgers psychologist says, it is inconceivable that one would buy a house before he had the money. In this country, however, people do it and then have to work more than one job to pay for it.

The fact is that, with easy credit and hard competition, many workers get trapped early into an occupation they do not like. Then, because of family responsibilities or just plain apathy, they are imprisoned there until they retire or die. They work for a paycheck and not for satisfaction. And the result is tension.

Why is work so unrewarding today? Why are we so often tense about it? First of all, according to the U.S. Department of Labor statistics, 80 percent of employed people in the United States are misemployed; they are working at the wrong jobs and doing things they are not proficient at doing. Therefore, they are tense. Secondly, there is an overemphasis on productivity, achievement, speed, and economic growth, while, at the same time, there is an underemphasis on individuality and self-satisfaction.

Dr. El-Meligi echoes many social psychologists when he maintains that our value system is dehumanizing. "There is an emphasis on productivity—the amount of work done everyday rather than in the long run. There is emphasis on getting things done quickly, so that if you don't make it by the time you are forty years old, it's over."

No wonder we are tense. We race against the clock, and most of the time we do it anonymously. Dr. El-Meligi says that experts are beginning to question the way we produce, from assembly lines to secretarial pools, in an effort to find ways to reduce tension and increase satisfaction. For instance, he says it is difficult for a secretary to work on an assignment when the five others next to her are all conversing.

"Americans tend to mass produce," he explains. "They are constantly seeking more efficient methods to put into effect." This tends to make workers automotons, he points out. But workers, unlike robots, have feelings and they must be able to feed back what they feel to management in order to obtain a sense of individual worth.

"Too often," the Rutgers professor says, "workers feel: 'I belong to the company. I make no decisions. There is no joy in doing my job. The company doesn't make me proud of who I am.' "

The uneasy question of: "Who am I? What's my purpose in life?" affects not only blue- and white-collar' workers but also top executives. Dr. Harry Levinson of the Levinson Institute in Cambridge, Massachusetts, says that executives want to look good to themselves and yet are under the constant threat of defeat. This creates severe tension. Many executives, even though they have achieved success, are under constant pressure not only from the competition, but also from the rapidly shifting marketplace, from internal rivalry, and other such strains which make their positions tenuous. Just as the old saying goes: "Uneasy lies the head that wears the crown," executives must guide and direct others. But they have difficulty depending upon others because they are continually fearful of losing power.

Dr. Levinson feels that perhaps America's top executives have it harder than executives in other nations because the former have much more social power. We have no traditional royalty or upper classes, so that highly paid company chiefs are the nobility. They are called upon to deal with social problems and community conflicts without either the preparation or the confidence to cope with them. Executives, he points out, are finding they have to justify what they are doing to their communities. Where once towns welcomed them or actively sought new industries, now company heads have to convince communities to allow their plants to locate there.

In addition, the Cambridge psychologist says that middle-management executives also have their crosses to bear. "They say: 'I'm tired of earning money for people who already have too much. What's in it for me?' They ask that not in the sense of monetary reward but in personal gratification."

"People have to have a flag to follow," Dr. Levinson maintains. "They have to have some reason to justify the expenditure of their lives in this activity." This is true not only of industry workers but also of housewives and mothers; they must have a sense of identity, of recognition, of satisfaction. In order to enjoy your job, it has to satisfy you, and in order to satisfy you, your work has to be recognized and appreciated by others. Do husbands really appreciate clean shirts, and do children appreciate healthful meals and a lot of chauffeuring? Many housewives and mothers don't think so.

The problem of recognition for work—any work—is particularly difficult today because few of us do a job from start to finish. Our jobs are anonymous and often quickly obsolete. There is just no permanent place in the sun for a large percentage of workers.

Is going back to a simpler time the answer? Many young people tried to do so in the 1960s by forming communes and getting "close to nature." But a study done by Dr. Joseph Eaton and Dr. Robert Weil at the University of Pittsburgh found that tension rears its ugly head among the plain living just as it does in the city and suburb. The two researchers discovered that among the American Hutterites, a separatist religious sect, removal of the stresses of modern urban society through life in a pastoral community with communal ownership of property does provide a system of basic security. However, this ordered life does not necessarily mean freedom from tension. The Hutterites have the same amount of tension and other emotional ills as the rest of us and are particularly prone to depressive disorders.

So what's the answer? How can you reduce tension at work and find more satisfaction in your job. First of all, according to the experts, you have to decide what you really want from work. Ask yourself: Is it a consistent, dependable income? Respect? Care during illness and a plan for retirement? Friends? Loyalty from fellow workers and your employer?

Do you want success and fame? The drive for success

and fame is usually based on the illusion that such recognition will increase your self-esteem and make other people respect you. But if that were entirely true, why are so many successful people so unhappy? Apparently success and fame do little for the inner person. No matter how much applause you get, if you are unable to think more of yourself consequently, it's not worth the sacrifice needed to obtain it.

So, you have to be sure of your goals—what you want for yourself and what you can achieve. Unfortunately, from the time you first entered school until today, you have let other people evaluate you. You have let other people tell you your skills, your disposition, your objectives. Now in order to be satisfied you have to learn to evaluate yourself.

Fortunately, thanks in a large part to the women's movement, it is not too late to change careers in midstream. There are many new opportunities for retraining for both men and women, and as a result you can have a second and even a third career.

Tension, as this book has pointed out before, occurs when no action is taken. So act now! The following are tried and true techniques for reducing tension at work:

Recognize there is no such thing as a tense job. You are tense, your job is not tense. It is how you react to the job. Other people may feel calm and collected while you feel overburdened. Why?

There is no such thing as overwork. Tension is created by faulty work habits. Sedentary jobs produce more tension than active ones, so take an exercise break. (See Chapter 7.)

Find out your real interests. Cut out everything from the newspaper that interests you for a month. Stack these articles all together, and then at the end of the month sort them according to interest. Try to determine why the subjects interested you. Then you will begin to see what your interests really are. Next you have to figure out how you can pursue them as a vocation.

List your goals. Sit down for thirty minutes. Think about your goals, and then list your lifetime goals in order of priority. List your yearly goals, your weekly goals, and tomorrow's goals—all in order of importance. This should give you a good idea of what you are really seeking. Always go after the most important things first. If you never get to the less important goals, so what!

Don't be afraid of failure. Try your best. Bypass obstacles when you can by taking the alternative. But tell yourself that everyone—yes, everyone—fails sometime, and it is better to have tried and failed than not to have tried at all.

Don't be a perfectionist. If you have to care for a house, do your major housecleaning in installments and relax your standards. No matter where you work, don't insist on perfection to the point where your progress is impeded and you can't produce. No one is perfect.

Write down your gripes. Write down all the things that have made you angry at work in the past six months. Once you have completed the list, look for a pattern. If you find one, think about how you can change it.

Be yourself. Don't try to change into someone else on the job. Form a clear idea of who you are and what you can do. Then do it.

Don't be afraid to refuse a promotion. If a promotion means you must move to a position you would find unfulfilling or one which you feel is beyond your ability to tolerate, don't take it. Many psychosomatic illnesses occur when a person is promoted to a job he or she feels inadequate to handle. Perhaps The Peter Principle *is* correct—that we are all promoted to the level of our maximum incompetence.

Don't make drastic changes on a new job. If you take a new job, get a clear idea of what is expected of you and what the company expects of all of its employees before you make any changes.

Establish credibility. This is important because you must have personal integrity so your subordinates and your employer can trust you.

Admit mistakes. You must be able to take risks and then benefit from your mistakes if you make them.

Don't feel that you are a symbol. You don't have to carry the burden of your sex, family, or ethnic group. You are yourself and represent yourself only.

Don't be afraid to complain. If you have an excessive work load, conflicting demands by superiors, or insufficient information for you to know what is required, say so. Those with repressed anger develop ulcers, tension headaches, and even heart attacks.

Skip the business lunch. If you feel tense when you conduct business over lunch and/or you tend to eat and drink too much, conduct your business at another time and take an exercise and/or rest break. (See Chapter 7.)

Plan your finances. Nothing can make you more tense than to have a lot of responsibilities and unpaid bills. Don't overspend so that you get trapped into working harder and harder and liking it less and less. Keep only two charge cards and throw the rest away so you won't be tempted to overuse credit. If you can't afford expert advice about your strained finances, go to your bank's trust department and to the library. Gather all the information you can, and then decide the best budget for you.

Set your retirement goals. Is early retirement possible? Are your goals realistic?

Be a good listener and a short answerer. When you are at work, really listen to what other people are saying; you will be able to deal with them more efficiently. Don't waste your time on small talk.

Set your watch ahead. Instead of lingering in bed until the last minute and then rushing to get to work, get up early enough to have breakfast and a leisurely trip to the office. Trying to beat the clock to appointments makes you tense, so allow yourself sufficient time. You can do this easily by setting your watch and clocks ahead by fifteen minutes.

Change your job. If you are unhappy in your work situation, sit down and have a real talk with yourself. What can you do about it? Can you change jobs? If so, do it. If not, try to figure out how you can make your work more enjoyable. It may take a professional to tell you how. Many unions, companies, and communities provide such experts for consultation.

Think of today. Today's work will not be too much of a burden for you if you do not add tomorrow's work to it. Think about what you have to do today and forget about your tasks for tomorrow. Tomorrow's work will then take care of itself.

5
Learn to Love Leisure

Why do you find it so hard to relax? Does doing nothing make you feel guilty? Are you compelled to justify your leisure by earning it?

If you really want to relieve your tension, you will have to learn to love leisure. If you don't, if you continue to ignore the balance between work and leisure, nature will do it for you. You will have a heart attack, ulcers, an accident, or some other surefire method will force you to slow down.

You have to accept the fact that you are mortal—you have only one life. You are not indispensable; you will eventually be replaced, so you may as well enjoy yourself—really enjoy yourself.

Certainly, leisure is just as necessary in your life as work. Without it you may succeed in your vocational goal, but the price you pay may be the loss of your family, your friends, and, ultimately, your health. Family, friends, and health all take time away from work.

How can you learn to love leisure? First of all, you have to realize that there is a difference between leisure and free time. Free time is the period you spend away from the nitty-gritty obligations that maintain your existence. Leisure, on the other hand, is freedom from imposed obligations upon your time. For instance, when you come home from work and you have free time before going to bed, you can spend it making repairs around the house or cutting the grass. You would then be using free time. But if, instead, you watch TV, play tennis, or indulge in a hobby because you want to, not because you must, you would be using leisure time.

Why do you have such difficulty with leisure? Why can't you just stop and smell a flower or sit back in a chair and take it easy? It may well be that you don't want to think; and during leisure, we really come into contact with ourselves.

Dr. Alexander Reid Martin, former chairman of the American Psychiatric Association's Standing Committee on Leisure, put it well when he observed: "Leisure is not the inevitable result of spare time, a holiday, weekend, or vacation. It is in the first place a particular state or condition of mind and being, specifically an actively receptive condition of the whole personality to open up to all stimuli from within and without. The personality is not passive or detached but wholly engaged in this process."

He explained that leisure is like physical relaxation and sleep. In all three states, the beginnings and duration are not subject to direct, conscious control but are determined unconsciously when outer and inner conditions are favorable. "Unfortunately," Dr. Martin said, "too many of us fear our unconscious. We are afraid of free association—the process of relaxing conscious control and expressing our thoughts and feelings spontaneously. Fear of the unconscious protects our illusions and Olympian aspirations, but it prevents us from feeling deeply. It perpetuates our avoidance of leisure and stifles all creative activity and growth."

Dr. Martin maintains that leisure is not the opposite of work in the sense of being opposed to work. "In work, there is a focusing, a contradiction of faculties, and the acuteness of consciousness. During leisure, there is an unfocusing, a relaxation of faculties, a greater diffusion of consciousness."

You may have to learn to let go of your work. Many psychotherapists recommend that you can do this by shifting your mind into a different image. For example, if you are working on a hard problem at the office, the mere fact that you are away won't take your mind off the job. But, you can force yourself to think about something else, such as a forthcoming party or your daughter's graduation. You will then replace the image of your work. In fact, this is one key to creativity.

According to Dr. Frederic F. Flach, associate clinical professor of psychiatry at Cornell University Medical

College, the source of creativity is in the preconscious. He explains that when we are conscious we are aware of our surroundings and are limited by the pedestrian, literal restrictions of conscious language. In our subconscious, our feelings are so buried that they are inaccessible. We have all those past painful experiences and emotions locked up tight.

However, in our preconscious, we keep things close to the surface. Here is our computer data center where we combine memories, fantasies, and the vibrations we pick up from other people. We are in touch with ourselves.

Dr. Flach adds that creativity usually involves an incubation period, especially if it includes an impasse. We put a problem in the back of our mind and then let it simmer. Suddenly, an hour, a day, or months later, the answer pops up. This is called "illumination." Then we go on to verify the solution and finally to employ the idea.

Everyone has had this experience. If you are a writer or a businessman, for instance, you may wake up in the middle of the night with the answer to something you thought had been put out of your mind. You can even learn to do this by forcing yourself to shift your thoughts to something less taxing when a solution eludes you or when you feel yourself becoming too tense. But make sure that what you shift to isn't going to make you as tense or more tense than before. For instance, some people play tennis or bridge with the same drive and intensity that they use to work—instead of shifting gears. Even with that great potential tension reliever, sex, some people are so intent on performing, so automatically committed to it, that the sexual experience creates, rather than releases, tension.

Our ability to relax, of course, is cultural and environmental. Right from the beginning we are patterned into a fast, speedy mold. We must be housebroken and ready for kindergarten at a certain age; we must graduate with our contemporaries. Each of us has to learn to be very competitive, and often the life pattern is set in early childhood. Consequently, we never know how to get off the carousel.

The Reverend John L. Thomas of Georgetown University's Jesuit Center for Social Studies in Washington, D.C., points out that in most other societies, even the industrialized ones, people are more adept at conversation. They seem to enjoy it. In Europe everyone spends a lot of time in coffeehouses or village pubs just in conversation and easy sharing.

Americans have trouble with such conversation. They find it difficult to justify what they think of as doing nothing or "just shooting the bull." But in relaxed conversations you do not get involved in intense discussions of politics, religion, or philosophy. You just enjoy each other as human beings; you communicate and relax.

Americans tend to sit, instead, in front of a television set for eighteen or twenty hours a week. Indeed, television can offer escape and therefore be a tension reliever. However, such use of leisure time tends to make a person somewhat passive and does not provide a wide range of free choice to discover and develop more satisfying spare time. What's more satisfying than TV?

One of the best means of really relaxing is to indulge in something you really like—a hobby, an activity apart from your main business. However, nowadays you never know when a hobby stops being strictly for fun and becomes a profession. Such a phenomenon is part of the American system.

In fact, hobbies can be very satisfying, especially if your work is tension producing, boring, or both. The ability to do something yourself from start to finish is good for your ego, providing, of course, that your hobby does not become an overpowering compulsion.

Some people become such fanatic collectors or sports buffs that the hobby becomes more stressful than work. Furthermore, when they are not working and cannot participate in their hobby, they are often at a loss as to what else to do with themselves.

Few people know how to choose or work at a hobby properly. Some select an activity that they don't really like because it is expected of them or is chic. Others choose a hobby that they cannot afford in time, money, or effort.

What hobby is best for you? There are four main hobby categories:

- Doing something
- Collecting things
- Learning things
- Making things

When selecting a hobby, ask yourself the following:

1. Will I be using different muscles and positions than I do at my work? For your hobby to be relaxing, you should.

2. Will it be too expensive or will the satisfaction be worth the cost?

3. Do I have the facilities for it—enough space? If I don't, how can I get enough?

4. Do I have enough ability for it? If you are tone deaf, it's rather foolish to take up the violin unless you hate your neighbors.

5. Can the ability be developed? Can I get the training? Where? When?

6. Is it safe? If it involves a fire hazard or special equipment, what precautions must I take? Is my eye sight good enough? What about my hearing, reflexes, and my patience?

7. Will it cause friction in the family?

8. Am I interested enough to keep at it or is it just a passing whim?

9. Is there anything else I might be more interested in—something that I used to want to do but have forgotten about?

10. Will it take up too much time and require more strength and energy than I have? If it is something I have done well in the past but not in recent years, am I sure I still have the strength that I know it requires?

If you want to find out more about a particular hobby, ask your local librarian for help. Practically every conceivable hobby has a book written about it and an organization made up of followers. Look in your local telephone directory or one of the almanacs to find local hobby clubs. Still another good source of information is the United States Government Printing Office, Washington, D.C. 20402. Booklets on various hobbies are offered for only a minimal fee.

Whether or not you opt for a hobby or for just doing nothing, get your life into balance. If you watch the ocean, you can see that it has a natural rhythm. A wave comes in and goes out, comes in and goes out. There should be a rhythm to your life too. If you work, relax, work, and relax, you can get more done and be healthier and more efficient. The relaxation break called "the weekend" was created just for that purpose. The change of seasons also provides a rhythm and a change of pace.

Remember, even God rested on the seventh day.

6
How to
Take a
Real
Vacation

Vacations are taken to give you a break in your routine, allow you to relax and have a good time. They are supposed to relieve tensions, give your body and mind a rest, and prepare you to face your daily life with renewed energy. That's what vacations are *supposed to do.*

But do you actually need a rest to recover from your vacation? Is it always a relief to get back to work after fighting traffic, crowds, high prices, and irritable relatives or friends?

If your vacation is not a safety valve which allows you to release inner tensions, then you had better sit down and plan one that really is. Fortunately for resorts and other tourists attractions, not everyone likes or needs the same type of vacation. It takes some people a week just to unwind, so for such people long vacations are in order. Others do well over long weekends and several small vacations a year.

The travelers who do twenty-two countries in fourteen days may be physically exhausted, it is true, but they may have the priceless benefits of a vacation just the same because they are away from their routine work and intent on something else.

Some individuals who are incurable workaholics must work even on vacations. And if they don't, more tension is created than if they had tried to relax. For them a working vacation may be more suitable. If they are in the medical field, for instance, they could be camp doctors or nurses. If they work in an office, they could take a temporary job at a resort. A number of vacationers worry continually about their jobs back home. And for them taking time off may cause more tension than if they had remained at work and just taken individual vacation days.

There is conflicting advice, even from the experts, about whether or not to take children on a vacation. Some say that parents should go alone and get to know each other again and obtain some relief from the responsibilities which exist in the home. Others say that it is a good idea to take the children along because it is a happy time, and the sharing of pleasant experiences strengthens family ties.

What about separate vacations for husbands and wives? Most social scientists frown upon it, as a general rule, unless there are extenuating circumstances. Such circumstances might be if a mate is incapacitated or has a different, unalterable vacation time. Psychologists feel that if a husband and wife do not want to vacation together, there is something wrong with the marriage. But suppose he wants a wilderness vacation and she likes to visit the big cities? It may be necessary to go to one type of vacation one year and another the next or to select a versatile spot which pleases both. Of course, this requires compromise which, in turn, requires maturity.

For some—and certainly not everyone—the most relaxing vacation is one in the outdoors, roughing it in a tent or a camper or just hiking on a trail. It is true that children can get bored in the wilderness, but according to outdoor expert Bill Dunlop, former president of the Society of American Travel Writers, this is because the mother and father do all the work and don't give the kids any responsibility. He thinks children should be in on things from the beginning: planning the trip, buying the food, gathering the supplies. The boys can do the cooking and the girls can dig the latrines and chop the wood. Fathers should not try to prove their superiority by doing everything, and mothers should not have to do the cooking or washing or any other chores they do at home.

In any event, everyone should vary their routine on a vacation. That's the purpose of taking time off. But any vacation requires careful planning. It may sound very romantic to be spontaneous, but if you arrive hot and tired in an area where you cannot obtain reservations, tension will rear its agitating head. And if you cannot find a bathroom or a restaurant for the children when they need it, anxiety increases.

But perhaps the biggest problem in vacation planning is unfulfilled expectations. Vacation periods can be, and in reality often are, times of damaging tension for you and yours. A spoiled vacation can be the result of faulty communications. Wives expect one thing, husbands another, and children still something else, and yet there is little discussion of these desires. To avoid these situations, you must begin your vacation plans well in advance of the time you are going to take off. The anticipation is an added value. Sit down when you make your plans and list everything you expect from the vacation. Each of those accompanying you on the trip should do the same. Once you set the plans, try to keep them. This keeps disappointments to a minimum.

Psychologists say that total isolation is not a good idea for most families. About seventy-two hours is the maximum one group can stay together exclusively and not build up tensions. People need escape hatches.

Visiting relatives for the entire vacation may also not be a good idea unless they have enough room and enough sense to give you some privacy.

How do you choose a relaxing vacation? Older people can have a very good time retracing their tracks. They can revisit the places they enjoyed while young, but they should always keep in mind that physically they have to take it easier than they did in the past.

Ideally, you should take a ten-day vacation every four months plus long weekends whenever possible. This routine is out of the question for most of us. However, there are some preparations and some precautions that everyone can take to make a vacation a real tension reliever:

• Take twice as much money and half the clothes you think you need. Nothing can make you more tense than to find you are running out of funds on a trip. And it is aggravating to lug around all those unnecessary clothes.

- Condition yourself before a trip which requires a time change. Once you arrive at your destination, do not plan anything until you have had a chance to rest up for twenty-four hours.

- If you wear glasses, carry an extra pair. And if you take regular medication, be sure of your supply before you leave.

- Know what sort of climate you will encounter at your vacation spot and dress accordingly. It can get cold in the mountains at night even in midsummer.

- Good walking shoes are one of the most important parts of your travel wardrobe. If your feet hurt, you can't be relaxed.

- Get your vaccinations early so you don't suffer a reaction while on vacation.

- Use common sense concerning your diet while traveling. Many a vacation has been spoiled by indiscreet eating and drinking. Avoid milk products and raw fruits and vegetables in most other countries except Western Europe and Canada.

- If you are traveling with children, be sure to bring a supply of things to keep them occupied. Rest frequently, eat at regular mealtimes, and take an extra change of clothes. Don't try to do too much at one time. Cranky children can create tremendous tension.

- Do not take work or material to study with you on vacation. Leave it all behind. Too many students and businessmen and women take their work with them and end up frustrated and ruining their vacation.

- Work variety into your vacations. Many people go to the same place each year. If you are content, do it. But it may be much more relaxing to explore new interests or vacation locations.

- Don't let your vacation time accrue. Make a point of using every bit of it.

● Each year allow enough time to do what you like to do and, as a result, you can avoid fatigue and frustration.

● If you are a workaholic, you'll have to learn to enjoy time off gradually. Begin by taking long weekends, say three or four days, then gradually build up to a week and then ten days.

● Come back from your vacation at least one day in advance. Too many people come rushing home at the last minute and then rush off to work.

● If you are going to choose a vacation home, select one no more than two hours' drive from your permanent house. It's nice to have a retreat, but if you retreat too far, it can cause stress instead of reducing it. Traffic is not going to get better.

● Start planning your next vacation as soon as you return from your current one.

7
Exercises
for
Relaxation

If you watch a cat watching a dog, what is the cat doing? The cat's back arches; its hair stands on end; it bares its teeth. The same sort of thing happens to us when we become tense. We feel it in the back of our necks and in our backs. Our muscles tighten—we are tense.

Tense muscles have been called our "body armor," or our "shield against the outside world." However, if we keep our armor on—if we find no relief—we wind up with a "tension headache," "a pain in the neck," a backache, or some other tension-related disability.

During our childhoods most of us have been discouraged from taking physical action when we are frustrated and tense. If we punched someone who bothered us, we got into trouble. But according to Dr. Max Novich of South Orange, New Jersey, an orthopedic surgeon, ex-boxer, and current specialist in sports medicine, that's why we grow up to be so "uptight." He believes we should stop saying "Don't fight" to children. And he maintains that if kids start hitting each other, we shouldn't put them in the corner, but in the gym with boxing gloves. We should let them slug it out.

"Aggression in a child is normal and is an instinctual force in growth and maturity," he explains. "It is linked to physical development and future individuality. If aggressiveness in children is turned inward, it can express itself as neurosis. A child who has learned to express his hostilities at home or school can face up to his opponents without suffering guilt."

Dr. Novich is all in favor of exercise, particularly contact sports, as a method of dealing with tension. "We analyze our adversary in a sport just as we prepare to meet the competition problems of living. As each new crisis arises, we execute the strategy we have planned. The disappointments and frustrations encountered in sports parallel those of life. In the frame of life, it takes a tremendous amount of courage, self-reliance, and confidence to 'come off the floor' and go on to victory."

Most contact sports are for the young. But everyone can benefit from exercise. Here are easy exercises that are designed specifically to relax tension. By unknotting your muscles, you can relax some of the psychic tension in your life.

Exercise 1

Lie on the floor with a small pillow under your head. Your knees should be slightly bent. Put one hand on your stomach and one hand on your chest. Draw deep breaths into your abdomen and feel it rise. Your chest should hardly move at all. Belly-breathe without your chest moving and, as you exhale through your nose, try to say "cheese." Do this exercise five times. Then take a deep breath, as deep as you can, and exhale saying "ha-a-a-a." Your jaw, tongue, and mouth should all be relaxed. Do this five times.

Hold your breath for thirty seconds. Then sigh deeply, letting all the air out of your lungs. Permit the air to return to your lungs naturally. Do this five times.

Exercise 2 (standing)

Stand with your knees slightly bent but not locked. Many tense people tend to lock their knees, which immobilizes the whole body. Take a position with your feet about eight inches apart and bend your knees so that the weight of your body is in balance between the heels and the balls of your feet. The rest of your body should be in a straight line with your arms hanging loosely at your side. Let your belly hang out. Don't force it out but don't hold it in either. Belly-breathe (see Exercise 1). Your back should be straight but not rigid, and your pelvis should be relaxed. Hold this position for two minutes.

When waiting in line or standing at a cocktail party, this is a relaxing stance. Try to keep it whenever you have to stand for any length of time.

Exercise 3 (standing)

Place your feet apart with your toes turned slightly inward. With your knees bent, bend over until your fingertips touch the floor. Then straighten your knees gradually until some shaking develops in your legs. Do not extend the knees fully and stiffen the legs, as this won't work. Have your mouth open slightly. All the time you are on your feet, your fingertips merely serve as points of contact. Hold position for the count of ten.

Exercise 4 (standing)

Stand as in Exercise 2 with your knees slightly bent. Then collapse and fold up like a doll on the floor. Be sure you do it slowly and that you use a carpeted floor or mat. Repeat three times.

Exercise 5

Stand or sit and extend your arms straight out from your shoulders. Then swing both arms around yourself in a hug, and then extend them out again. Alternate putting your right arm over your left in the hug and then your left arm over your right. Do this with wild abandon ten times.

Exercise 6 (sitting)

No matter where you are—at your desk, in a meeting, at home—you can do this exercise unobtrusively. Wriggle your toes, giving special attention to your big toes for one minute. Then circle your feet by rotating them on your ankles. Next tighten your buttocks, count to five, and then relax. Tighten your stomach muscles, count to five, and relax. Inhale deeply into your abdomen and then exhale slowly. Not only will you relax—your shape will shape up. This is a good exercise to do everytime a TV commercial comes on the screen.

Exercise 7 (sitting)

Take a deep breath, raise your arms to shoulder height and stretch your fingers until you can feel a pull in the fourth and fifth. Exhale as you lower your arms to your side. Then inhale as you lift your arms so they meet above your head. This gives you a feeling of soaring. Exhale as you lower your arms to your side. Do these two arm exercises five times.

Exercise 8 (sitting)

Turn your head to the right slowly. Turn your head to the left slowly. Bend your head back slowly. Bend your head forward slowly. Then turn your head and shoulders to the left and then to the right. Bend back slightly and then forward at your waist. Raise your right shoulder and let it drop. Raise your left shoulder and let it drop. Raise both shoulders while you bend your head backward. This is a great tension reliever for people who bend over a desk or worktable all day.

Exercise 9 (sitting)

While you are sitting, put your hands on the arms of the chair or on the seat of the chair and do a chair push-up—raise your body off the chair with your hands. By doing this, you will use the muscles that are the exact opposite of the ones which become taut when you are tense. This counteracts the tension in those muscles.

Exercise 10 (sitting)

Bring your right knee up to your chin. Put it down. Bring your left knee up to your chin. Put it down. Point your left knee out to the side and then put it in its normal forward position. Do the same thing with your right knee. Repeat five times.

Exercise 11 (sitting)

Each time you feel yourself getting tense, squeeze your fists. If you have long nails, you can put something into your hands. By making your fists as tight as possible, and then relaxing your hands, you will feel more relaxed. This is a terrific exercise if you get really angry at someone; it helps you maintain control.

Exercise 12 (sitting)

Sit straight in your chair with your knees about ten inches apart and your legs slanting slightly forward. Then let yourself collapse like a rag doll into your lap with your head forward and your spine rounded. Close your eyes and imagine that your eyes are so loose that they are going to fall out. Let your jaw hang open. Rest your hands on your knees. Check yourself to be sure you are comfortable and then tell yourself that your right arm is heavy . . . your right arm is heavy . . . your right arm is heavy. Repeat this twenty times while concentrating on your arm from armpit to fingertips. Then make a fist, flex your arms, take a deep breath, and open your eyes. After you become adept at making your right arm heavy, you can extend the heaviness to your left arm, your legs, and your whole body, until you are able to relax from head to toe.

Exercise 13 (sitting)

Bend your head forward with your eyes closed. Imagine your eyes are so loose that they are going to fall out of your head. Let your jaw hang open, and rest your chin on your chest. Take a deep breath, hold it, and begin to rotate your head slowly around to the right, all the way back, and let your head fall back on your shoulder. Then exhale and rest. Start the same procedure to the left and rotate in the same way. Take a deep breath, hold it, and raise your right shoulder. Roll your shoulder forward, up, back, and around in a complete circle. Exhale. Do the same thing with your left shoulder. This is a tension reliever for people who suffer from tension headaches and/or stiff necks.

Exercise 14 (standing or sitting)

Do this fast exercise whenever you can, wherever you are, whether sitting or standing. Look up at the ceiling or sky while raising both shoulders at the same time. This is also good for those prone to tension headaches, shoulder pains, and neck aches. Do this exercise five times whenever you feel yourself getting tense.

Exercise 15 (standing or sitting)

Stand up or sit up straight and look at the ceiling or sky. Smile and then blow an imaginary bubble high into the air. Repeat your smile and bubble blowing five times. This is another exercise which loosens the neck, shoulder, and facial muscles tightened during tension.

Exercise 16 (underwater)

In the bathtub or swimming pool, wiggle your toes underwater, one foot at a time and then both feet together. Roll each foot around in a circle clockwise and then counterclockwise. Flex each knee a few times. Shift your weight from side to side on your buttocks. Roll your submerged wrists in both directions. Bend and straighten each arm underwater. Roll each shoulder around from front to back. Turn around and with your face in the water blow bubbles. Do this three times.

There are two other exercises which are so often recommended for the relief of tension that we sort of take them for granted. But they are, indeed, two of the very best tension relievers.

Take a walk. Walking is an easy kind of exercise, but it uses a variety of muscles. It offers tranquility, especially if you walk in a lovely or interesting place. If you have to force yourself to walk, do so by parking your car a considerable distance from your destination. For instance, if you have to go to the supermarket, park a half a mile away if you can. Walking around a shopping center can give your arms and legs a lot of exercise while you concentrate on other things.

Jog. Jogging has been called yoga in motion. You should not do it unless you have received an O.K. from your physician. It gives you a feeling of serenity and peace if you run at a rhythmic pace. Jogging is good exercise and a wonderful way to let off steam because, as has been pointed out in this book a number of times, our bodies were made for flight when stress occurs. And jogging is controlled flight.

8
Coping

Tension is a part of living; it can be a spice or a poison depending upon how you cope with it. To cope means to "contend with successfully."

What makes one person better able to cope with stress than another? A study of the eighty-two surviving members of the U.S.S. *Pueblo* crew, which was subjected to eleven months of ill treatment by the North Koreans, resulted in some interesting findings. Researchers compared the crew members who withstood the stress well to those who did not. They found no correlation among social backgrounds, education, or religious beliefs. The men who coped had a wide variety of ego defenses, including humor, faith, reality testing, denial, rationalization, and the ability to utilize fantasy.

Fortunately, you will probably not have to undergo the tremendous stress to which the *Pueblo* crew was subjected. But still, how you handle your tensions is important to you and your health.

You can learn to counteract the emotional and biological stress initially designed for fight or flight. And, you can do this without pills, alcohol, or blaming others.

The following techniques have been culled from the advice of many experts. These methods have all been successful in reducing tension. However, since what makes you tense is strictly personal, some will work for you and some won't. Test them and keep testing until you develop your own surefire system of coping with tension.

Don't let things drift. If there are undercurrents of unhappiness or tension in your life, do something about it. Tension is a signal and requires action.

Find out what you are afraid of. Sometimes fear itself is what is fearful. Have a talk with yourself. Confront your fears and admit them. Once you identify what's really bothering you, you can do something about it.

Don't blame others. Blaming others is almost a reflex when something goes wrong. You have to be able to identify the problem when it appears in order to control it more effectively. To get some perspective or objectivity is difficult; in fact, it is a lifetime project. But you have to begin sometime to take responsibility for yourself.

Live your life to be comfortable. It is easy to get brief happiness by avoiding troubles and situations which might cause discomfort or by cutting off relationships which are difficult and perhaps painful, but trying to sidestep tension is never a long-term solution. You have to deal with it, and be willing to risk discomfort and unhappiness to achieve your goal of emotional satisfaction, of which happiness is a natural by-product.

Do something for others. The ungiving self is the unfulfilled self. If you are helping others and concentrating on their problems, it is hard to worry about your own. There is a great need for your services. There is need for foster grandparents, volunteers in mental hospitals, Red Cross drivers, teacher's aides, and friendly visitors to name just a few. And don't forget political campaigns and scouting. There is an endless variety from which you can choose.

Arrange for privacy. Everyone should have someplace where he or she can be alone. You need to be able to get off and relax and think without interruption—without other people making demands upon your attention. This is particularly important for mothers of small children. Privacy is just as necessary as work, sleep, and food.

Don't stick to a problem. Sometimes sticking with a problem prevents you from finding the answer, and it can be a form of self-punishment. The old idea of concentrating on a problem until it is resolved is now considered unwise. Get away for a while and think about other things. You may well find that the solution appears like magic while you are doing something else or as soon as you get back to the problem itself.

Make a decision. It is better to make the wrong decision than to avoid making a decision at all. You have to decide *now* whether it will be A or B. Anybody can think of good reasons on both sides. But if you wait for 100-percent assurance, you'll wait forever. So make up your mind. Make the decision and carry it out. An error can be corrected, but indecision allows tension to linger until you are worn out.

Don't overdo the details. Details can be completed, but sometimes a concern about small things leads to smallness in thinking. Some people become tense because they drown in their own details and then get pulled every which way worrying about them.

Don't insist on winning. Everybody loses sometime and you are no different than anyone else. Sometimes we benefit more by losing and trying again, then by winning.

Even when you're right, give in. You may be right, but proving it may not be worth it. You can win the battle but lose the war and no one likes someone who is always right.

Don't play a role. If you select a role such as "the man in the gray flannel suit" or the "superefficient housewife," you can get locked in, and you can't do things another way. Be flexible. Don't pretend.

Own up to who you are. Stop trying to make the whole world love you. Stop trying to control the whole world. If you stop such neurotic behavior, you will be less tense and happier.

Don't judge yourself sternly. Don't expect more of yourself than others. It sounds like a fine idea to hold yourself up as a better model, but this is the road to tension, ulcers, headaches, and backaches. Accept yourself with your faults.

Respect yourself. It is better to have a high opinion of yourself and be accused of being egotistical than a low opinion of yourself and find that others accept your own evaluation. A person might believe that he is really unworthy of success or acceptance. That is the road to depression and tension.

Compromise. Acting on principle is fine, but sometimes refusal to yield because of the "principle of the thing" becomes indistinguishable from stubbornness. Compromise is essential to almost all human relationships. Rigid structures break easily. Flexibility is not only desirable to avoid tension but it is also practical; it gets things done.

Don't do wrong. If you know it is wrong, don't do it. Normal people get guilt feelings that way and feelings of guilt are hard to live with and lead to brooding, self-recrimination, and, of course, tension.

Don't wait for the sword to fall. If you are anxious about something and you can't talk yourself out of the anxiety, try to advance the event that is making you tense so that the anticipated occasion comes and goes. Note that you survived the event and think about that the next time you are worried about a future occurrence.

Find security. You can't help but be tense if you are worried about survival. Indeed, this takes priority over most other things. You need to find someone on whom you can depend emotionally. You have to find a way to pay for the necessities.

Be healthy. Attitudes toward health should be realistic. You should have a personal physician for when you become ill, and you should have periodic health maintenance examinations. Promptly report any new or persistent symptoms which develop between exams. Worrying about the symptom can make you tense.

Respect your body. You can't feel free of tension if you are malnourished, ill, or overly tired. Improvement in your physical health can bring marked improvement in your ability to cope with stress.

Get sufficient sleep. Everyone has his or her own personal sleep needs, whether it is four hours or ten a night. Find out just how much sleep is necessary for you and then get it. Everyone—but everyone—is tense when fatigued.

Relax as soon as you are fatigued. You should, as soon as you feel fatigued, relax. If you wait until you are completely exhausted, you will be tense and it will be more difficult for you to recuperate. For most people the best times to take a relaxation break are just before lunch, in the evening before dinner, and when going to bed. See Chapters 3 and 7 for relaxation techniques.

Take one thing at a time. You can only do one thing at a time, so select the most important task and get to work on it. Proceed step by step in descending order of importance. The other problems can wait. If you worry about all you have to do, you'll become tense and inefficient.

Change your environment. If you find tension building up without relief, it may be time to change your environment for a while. Go to a new site, travel, or just change rooms in your own house.

Change your routine. Routine can be boring and thus tension-producing. Change the way you walk to school or travel to work. Use a different supermarket. Do the things at night that you ordinarily do in the daytime. Have your lunch at suppertime and supper at lunch. Do anything, but change your routine.

Don't overcompete. Competition is contagious at work, in school, during sports—but so is cooperation. When you become a little less competitive toward the other person, you often make it easier for yourself. If your opponent no longer feels you are a threat, he or she becomes much less of a threat to you.

Work off your anger. If you are really angry, take a walk, punch your pillow, do some physical labor. Physical exercise can be the most efficient method of working off the tension caused by anger.

Don't be overeager. Eagerness and zest are charming traits, but don't go overboard. Unbounded enthusiasm makes people think you are hasty. Bubbly stuff often evaporates quickly.

Talk to a friend. Even if your friend can't give you expert advice, talking to someone—the very act of getting it off your chest—can help you. If you do not want to reveal your problems to a friend, then talk into a tape recorder or write your problems down. This will help you put things in focus.

Choose your associates carefully. If you associate with people who are constantly tearing you down, criticizing you, you will be inefficient and unhappy. Seek out the people who are constructive, not destructive.

Make overtures. Don't sit around waiting to be asked. Go out and greet the world, but don't overdo it. That can lead to rejection. But there is a middle ground, and you have to be somewhat of a pioneer to find it. There are other people out there who would like to be with you but haven't met you yet. Go out and meet them. Professional societies, sports groups, churches, charity organizations, town meetings and political organizations all offer events which can lead to companionship.

Get involved. If things are happening in your community that don't involve you, get involved, for being involved in the world around you is one of the secrets of keeping alive and well. When older people start to withdraw from the world, they begin to die a little. You should get involved in what is going on in the schools, the streets, city hall, and other places where the action is and where decisions are being made.

Be reasonable about work and leisure. Everyone needs both work and leisure, but not everybody enjoys a job. Adopt the attitude that any assignment is a challenge, something you must do whether you like it or not. Evaluate your work and daily routine carefully; hard work alone is almost never responsible for tension. Everyone should have a number of sources of satisfaction to pursue in leisure time.

Music hath charms. Music is a powerful tool. It should never be played continuously, but for only twenty to forty minutes at a stretch. And it should be played on good equipment, because scratchy noises and poor fidelity can cause fatigue and irritation. If you are in a bad mood, start out with melancholy tones and gradually change to cheerful, lively music. If you are agitated and tense, start out with lively music and then go to slow, soothing melodies.

Read a book. This sounds simplistic, but television, while an easy diversion, cannot place you in another world in the same way a book can. If you select a book in which you are really interested—one you can't put down—you can escape and relax.

Take a warm bath. Even the ancient Romans knew about hydrotherapy. Take a warm bath. Add some sweet-smelling oil or bath salts to the water, lie back, and relax. Lying in warm water for half an hour is one of the best methods of relaxing.

Get a massage. Manipulating tension-knotted muscles relaxes them and therefore relaxes you. If you can't afford a professional masseur or masseuse, a relative or friend can learn massage. There are a number of books on the market which give instructions. If no one is available, massage yourself. Starting with your toes, work your way up to your neck, kneading your muscles as you go. Use a scented lotion.

Solve puzzles. Jigsaw, crossword, and other puzzles offer a means of finding solutions. When you solve a puzzle, it gives you emotional satisfaction and the encouragement that you will be able to solve life's puzzles.

Swim: Just as taking a warm bath is relaxing, swimming can reduce tensions. Both involve water and a return to a womblike environment. Swimming provides exercise and at the same time supports your body, giving you a subliminal feeling of security.

Seek humor. Humor is not a fixed commodity; it reflects society. But humor is man's built-in tranquilizer. It usually involves a problem which is solved in an incongruous or surprising manner. In the middle of something very serious or very tense, people are still able to laugh. Freud said humor is used to express our socially unacceptable impulses in a socially acceptable way. In a crisis situation, if you can laugh at something silly, it can be a great tension reliever. Try to find a new perspective in the situation—the incongruities. There are countless joke books. Find one with the subject matter that is making you tense—even if it is death or sickness. By reading about your worries in a humor book, tension can be relieved. Actually, humor really is only making light of serious situations.

Brush your hair. By brushing your hair in slow, even strokes or by massaging your scalp, you will increase the circulation and reduce the tightness in those muscles frequently affected by tension—the scalp, forehead, and neck muscles. Perform at least fifty strokes.

Bake bread. Aside from the soothing, delicious odor and the satisfaction of doing something so basic for yourself, baking bread is very soothing. Kneading the dough is a great way to work off tension. The more you slam and push and punch the dough around, the better your bread will be and the better you will feel.

Make your desires clear. Be willing to say what you want and don't want and what you are willing and not willing to do. Don't make people guess. Don't disguise your true feelings. If you say "yes" when you mean "yes" and "no" when you mean "no," you will avoid a great deal of tension.

Learn to listen to what you are saying. You can tell a lot about yourself if you really listen to what you are saying to others. Why did you say that? What do you mean? When do you first begin to feel tense in that situation? You can analyze yourself if you sit down and take the time to do it.

Analyze your pet peeves. We all have pet peeves— those certain things that should be inconsequential but which make us physically and emotionally tense all out of proportion. Try to trace back to the root of the pet peeve. If you can remember why you become tense in that particular situation, you can learn a great deal about yourself, and you can control your reaction.

Pretend you are not tense. Sometimes if you act as if you are not tense and picture yourself in some idyllic spot, you relax. This does not always work, but it's worth a try. Deliberately relax each group of muscles, put a smile on your face, and pretend.

Find your stress level. You are an individual. We all are. Each of us is influenced by heredity, predispositions, and the expectations of our society. However, if you can find your own personal stress point, the point at which you are most efficient, you can succeed and be happy. If you go over that point, you may develop harmful tension. If you go under it, you will not achieve your potential. Stay right on target.

Stop making excuses. The "if onlys" and the "I would have buts" never do any good. You can't change your parents, the place of your birth, your brothers and sisters, or your talents. You are responsible for yourself and for your own abilities. Take action.

Correct your mistakes. One of the great human gifts is the ability to keep correcting oneself throughout life. Every human makes mistakes. You can apologize, right your wrongs, try again. You can change and become more skillful.

Go for mental health advice. What's the difference between receiving therapy for an ulcer, migraine, or heart attack and receiving therapy for the underlying emotional disorder that caused the harmful symptoms in the first place? There is no more disgrace in going to a mental health therapist than there is going to any other physician. You may need just one visit or a number of visits with a professional who can help you analyze your stressful situation, pinpoint the source of your tension, and offer you methods for solving your problems. (See page 86.)

Learn to live for today. It's the "what ifs" and the "suppose this happens" that create tension. You can take care of today if you don't try to add tomorrow to it. Forget the past; it's gone, and all the power in the world won't bring it back. Deal only with the present, not tomorrow or yesterday.

Be realistic. You have to accept the fact that certain things are in your power and certain things are not. Stop frustrating yourself by going after the impossible. The key to a healthy life, therefore, is balance. If you go too far in any direction, you violate reality. Reality is not only a matter of dealing with the present but of being aware that life is always a compromise. You have to find the middle ground.

Your goal is to achieve and maintain mental and physical health. As this book has pointed out over and over again, these two are interrelated. We all know what physical health is, but mental health is harder to explain. One of its classic concepts has been described by Dr. Marie Jahoda in *Current Concepts in Mental Health,* published in 1958. She described the mentally healthy person as:

1. Self-aware, self-accepting, and with a sense of identity.

2. Open to growth and to the modification of one's disease.

3. Having an integrated personality, which implies consistency and resistance to stress.

4. Autonomous—having the ability to act independently and make one's own decisions.

5. Having an undistorted perception of reality, which includes both "realism" and sensitivity to other people's feelings.

6. Being able to master one's environment, which includes having the ability to love, to solve problems when they are encountered, and to engage in practical work.

Remember, we all need some tension in our life to make it interesting. We still need the desire to survive, but we need to adapt to it. As the scientist-philosopher René Dubos of Rockefeller University has said: "Step by step we are removing so much of our freedom to express our being, as human being from other human beings—our individuality, that single quality that makes man different from man. We are unquestionably breeding men best suited to perform in an environment where the condition for survival is conformity. The greatest problem that will face our crowded communities will not be disease but that we will become so adapted to the conditions we are creating that we will accept or welcome treeless pavements under starless skies in a spring without the song of birds."

The threat of such a stressless life has led Dr. Dubos to urge that tension be controlled, not eliminated. "Without exposure and response to stress," he concludes, "any organism—man in particular—stays where he is. All of biological history demonstrates without doubt that an organism too neatly adapted to too well-defined conditions has no chance in the long run. Unless he is capable of responding to change he will surely be displaced by another creature."

Some things happen to us in life over which we have little control. Drs. Thomas H. Holmes and Richard H. Rahe, of the University of Washington Medical School, developed the following scale for measuring stress in terms of "life events." They say a person scoring less than 150 on their scale has only a 37 percent chance of becoming ill during the next two years. A score of 150 to 300 raises the odds to 51 percent, and a 300-plus score means you have an 80 percent chance of becoming seriously ill. Check the list below and consider the events in your own life for the past twelve months. Fill in the amount given for each, and add up the total. No matter what it is, you can do something to counteract the stress. The first step is to be aware that you are tense. The next is to do something about it. There are many actions described in this book which are proven tension fighters. It's up to you to make use of them in your life.

Life Events Stress Quiz

Rank event	Value your score
1. Death of spouse	100 _____
2. Divorce	73 _____
3. Marital separation	65 _____

Rank Event   **Value Your Score**

 4. Jail term   63 _____
 5. Death of close family member   63 _____
 6. Personal injury or illness   53 _____
 7. Marriage   50 _____
 8. Fired from work   47 _____
 9. Marital reconciliation   45 _____
10. Retirement   45 _____
11. Change in family member's health   44 _____
12. Pregnancy   40 _____
13. Sex difficulties   39 _____
14. Addition to family   39 _____
15. Business readjustment   39 _____
16. Change in financial status   38 _____
17. Death of close friend   37 _____
18. Change to different line of work   38 _____
19. Change in number of marital arguments   35 _____
20. Mortgage or loan over $10,000   31 _____
21. Foreclosure of mortgage or loan   30 _____
22. Change in work responsibilities   29 _____
23. Son or daughter leaving home   29 _____
24. Trouble with in-laws   29 _____
25. Outstanding personal achievement   28 _____
26. Spouse begins or stops work   26 _____
27. Starting or finishing school   26 _____
28. Change in living conditions   25 _____
29. Revision of personal habits   24 _____
30. Trouble with boss   23 _____
31. Change in work hours, conditions   20 _____
32. Change in residence   20 _____
33. Change in schools   20 _____
34. Change in recreational habits   19 _____
35. Change in church activities   19 _____
36. Change in social activities   18 _____
37. Mortgage or loan under $10,000   17 _____
38. Change in sleeping habits   16 _____
39. Change in number of family gatherings   15 _____

Rank Event	Value	Your Score
40. Change in eating habits	15	_____
41. Vacation	13	_____
42. Christmas season	12	_____
43. Minor violation of the law	11	_____
Total		_____

Additional Readings
and Resources

Mental Health Associations

American Psychiatric Association
  1700 18th Street, N. W.
  Washington D. C. 20009.

American Psychological Association
  1200 17th Street, N. W.
  Washington D. C. 20009.

National Association for Mental Health
  1800 N. Kent Street
  Arlington, Virginia 22209.

National Institute of Mental Health
  5600 Fishers Lane
  Rockville, Maryland 20852.

Selected Readings

Robert Ader, Ph.D., "Effects of Early Experience and Differential Housing on Susceptibility to Gastric Erosions in Lesion-Susceptible Rats," *Psychosomatic Medicine*, Vol. 32, No. 6 (November–December 1970), pp. 569–579.

Robert Ader, Ph.D., "The Role of Developmental Factors in Susceptibility to Disease," *Current Trends in Psychosomatic Medicine* (1970), pp. 2–20.

Robert Ader, Ph.D., "The Significance of Early Life Experiences for the Study of Development," *Psychiatria, Neurologia, Neurochirurgia* (Amsterdam), Vol. 75 (1972), pp. 79–80.

Franz Alexander, "Physiologic Concomitants of Psychic Conflict," *The Story of Psychosomatic Medicine #3*, Hoffmann-La Roche Inc., 1975.

James C. Ascough and Carl N. Sipprelle, "Operant Verbal Conditioning of Autonomic Responses," *Behavior, Research & Therapy*, Vol. 6 (1968), pp. 363–370.

James R. Averille, "Personal Control over Aversive Stimuli and Its Relationship to Stress," *Psychological Bulletin*, Vol. 80, No. 4 (1973), pp. 286–303.

John F. Beary, B.S., Herbert Benson, M.D., Helen P. Klemchuk, A.B., "A Simple Psychophysiologic Technique Which Elicits the Hypometabolic Changes of the Relaxation Response," *Psychosomatic Medicine*, Vol. 36, No. 2 (March–April 1974), pp. 115–119.

Henry K. Beecher, M.D., "Non-Specific Forces Surrounding Disease and the Treatment of Disease," The Anaesthesia Laboratory of Harvard Medical School at the Massachusetts General Hospital, Boston, 1961, pp. 1–14.

Herbert Benson, M.D., John F. Beary, B.S., Mark P. Carol, "The Relaxation Response," *Psychiatry*, Vol. 37 (February 1974), pp. 37–45.

Frank M. Berger, M.D., "The Tranquilizer Decade," *A Symposium on Anxiety and a Decade of Tranquilizer Therapy*, New York, April 1, 1964.

Philip H. Bornstein and Carl N. Sipprelle, "Case Histories and Shorter Communications: Group Treatment of Obesity by Induced Anxiety," *Behavior, Research & Therapy*, Vol. 11 (1973), pp. 339–341.

Philip H. Bornstein and Carl N. Sipprelle, "Induced Anxiety in the Treatment of Obesity: A Preliminary Case

Report," *Behavior Therapy*, Vol. 4, No. 1 (January 1973), pp. 141–143.

Alexis Brook, M.B., M.R.C. Psych., D.P.M., "Mental Stress at Work," *The Practitioner*, Vol. 210 (April 1973), pp. 500–506.

Walter B. Cannon, "The 'Fight' or 'Flight' Principle," *The Story of Psychosomatic Medicine #1*, Hoffmann-La-Roche Inc., 1968.

George M. Carstairs, "Mental Health—What Is It?" *World Health*, May 1973, p. 8.

Peter T. Chew, "Workaholics Fidget Away Vacations," *The National Observer*, June 30, 1973.

Robert Coursey, "Biofeedback Machines: Their Problems and Potential," interview with author courtesy of the University of Maryland Public Relations Department, February 1975.

Hartvig Dahl and Donald P. Spence, "Mean Heart Rate Predicted By Task Demand Characteristics," *Psychophysiology*, Vol. 7, No. 3 (1971), pp. 369–376.

Dr. René Dubos, "The Tensions Around Us," *Modern Medicine*, January 20, 1964.

Dr. A. Moneim El-Meligi, Professor of Organizational Psychology at Rutgers Graduate School of Business Administration, interview with author, Newark, N.J., June 3, 1974.

George L. Engel, M.D., and Robert Ader, Ph.D., "Psychological Factors in Organic Disease," *National Institute of Mental Health Report*, October 1967.

"Facts About the Mental Health of Children," National Institute of Mental Health, U.S. Department of Health, Education and Welfare, No. (HSM) 72-9147, 1972.

Dana L. Farnsworth, M.D., "Emotional Problems of College Students," *Feelings and Their Medical Significance*, Ross Laboratories, 1964.

Helmuth Fichtler and Robert R. Zimmermann, "Changes in Reported Pain from Tension Headaches," *Perceptual and Motor Skills*, Vol. 36, No. 712 (1973).

Sol L. Garfield, Samuel Gershon, Ivan Sletten, Donald M. Sundland, and Susan Ballou, "Chemically Induced Anxiety," *International Journal of Neuropsychiatry*, 3(5) (1967), pp. 426–433.

Benson E. Ginsburg, Ph.D., "Heredity's Effect on Behavior Under Stress," National Institute of Mental Health, 1967, pp. 89–94.

Nancy Israel Goldberger and Paul L. Wachtel, "Hypnotizability and Cognitive Controls," *The International Journal of Clinical and Experimental Hypnosis*, Vol. XXI, No. 4 (1973), pp. 298–304.

Alvin F. Goldfarb, M.D., "Menstrual Problems—The Female Cycle Is Sensitive to the Stresses and Upheavals of Daily Living," *Sexual Behavior*, January 1973, pp. 17–21.

Elmer E. Green and Alyce M. Green, "Volition as a Metaforce in Psychophysiological Self-Regulation," Sixth Annual Medical Meeting of the Association for Research and Enlightenment, Phoenix, Arizona, January 14, 1973, pp. 1–20.

Elmer E. Green, Alyce M. Green, and E. Dale Walters, "Biofeedback Training for Anxiety Tension Reduction," Research Department, The Menninger Foundation, May 15, 1973, pp. 1–8.

William A. Greene, M.D., Elizabeth K. Speegle, M.S.N., Nancy Littlefield, B.A., Rue L. Cromwell, Ph.D., John J. DeCamilla, B.S., and Arthur J. Moss, M.D., "Psychosocial and Physiological Variables Associated with Affect States Following Acute Coronary Events," American Psychosomatic Society presentation, March 21, 1975, pp. 1–7.

Roy R. Grinker, Sr., M.D., and Beatrice Werble, Ph.D., "Mentally Healthy Young Men (Homoclites) 14 Years Later," *Archives of General Psychiatry*, Vol. 30 (May 1974), pp. 701–704.

Ernest Harburg, Ph.D., John C. Erfurt, B.A., Louise S. Hauenstein, Ph.D., Catherine Chape, M.A., William J. Schull, Ph.D., and M. A. Schork, Ph.D., "Socio-Ecological Stress, Suppressed Hostility, Skin Color, and Black–White Male Blood Pressure: Detroit," *Psychosomatic Medicine*, Vol. 35, No. 4 (July–August 1973), pp. 276–296.

Ernest R. Hilgard, "Developmental-Interactive Aspects of Hypnosis," *HEW Grant Abstract*, 1972.

August B. Hollingshead, Ph.D., "Environmental Stress and Schizophrenia," *National Institute of Mental Health Report*, October 1, 1965, pp. 241–243.

Robert R. Holt, "On the Interpersonal and Intrapersonal Consequences of Expressing or Not Expressing Anger," *Journal of Consulting and Clinical Psychology*, Vol. 35, No. 1 (1970), pp. 8–12.

"How Tension Builds," *Patterns of Tension #1*, Hoffmann-La Roche Inc., 1975.

"How You Can Handle Pressure," National Institute of Mental Health, U.S. Department of Health, Education and Welfare, No. (ADM) 74-21, 1973.

Martin A. Jacobs, Ph.D., Aron Z. Spilken, M.A., Martin M. Norman, M.A., and Luleen S. Anderson, Ph.D., "Life Stress and Respiratory Illness," *Psychosomatic Medicine*, Vol. 32, No. 3 (May–June 1970), pp. 233–241.

Martin A. Jacobs, Aron Z. Spilken, Martin M. Norman, and Luleen S. Anderson, "Patterns of Maladaptation and Respiratory Illness," *Journal of Psychosomatic Research*, Vol. 15 (1971), pp. 63–72.

Martin A. Jacobs, Aron Z. Spilken, Martin M. Norman, Luleen Anderson, and Eliyahu Rosenheim, "Perceptions of Faulty Parent–Child Relationships and Illness Behavior," *Journal of Consulting and Clinical Psychology*, Vol. 39, No. 1 (1972), pp. 49–55.

Russ Jalbert, Oakland Financial Group, interview with author, December 2, 1973 on family finances.

Irmis Johnson, "Easy Ways to Relieve Tension," *The American Weekly*, November 11, 1962.

Charles S. Jordan and Carl N. Sipprelle, "Physiological Correlates of Induced Anxiety with Normal Subjects," *Psychotherapy: Theory, Research and Practice*, Vol. 9, No. 1 (Spring 1972), pp. 18–21.

Dr. Margaret Kenrick, Chairman and Director of Physical Medicine and Rehabilitation at Georgetown

University, interview on relaxation courtesy of Georgetown University Public Relations Department, Washington, D.C., 1974.

Peter J. Lang, Ph.D., "Acquisition of Heart Rate Control: Method, Theory, and Clinical Implications," *Clinical Applications of Psychophysiology* (in press).

Peter J. Lang, Ph.D., "Learned Control of Human Heart Rate in a Computer-Directed Environment," *Cardiovascular Psychophysiology* (1974), pp. 392–405.

Peter J. Lang, Ph.D., "The On-Line Computer in Behavior Therapy Research," *American Psychologist*, No. 24 (1969), pp. 236–239.

Peter J. Lang, Ph.D., William G. Troyer, Jr., M.D., Craig T. Twentyman, M.S., Robert J. Gatchel, Ph.D., "Differential Effects of Heart Rate Modification Training on College Students, Older Males, and Patients with Ischemic Heart Disease," University of Wisconsin, 1974.

Chauncey D. Leake, Ph.D., "A Symposium on Anxiety and a Decade of Tranquilizer Therapy," New York, April 1, 1964.

"Learning to Relax Is Important to Your Health," news release from the American Medical Association, July 1967, pp. 1–5.

Harry Levinson, Ph.D., "A Psychoanalytic View of Occupational Stress," Occupational Stress Conference of the Center for Occupational Mental Health, September 23, 1972.

Harry Levinson, Ph.D., "Dilemmas of Top Management:

A Psychoanalytic Point of View," the Institute for Psychoanalysis, Chicago, Illinois, November 30, 1973.

Jesse A. Mann, Ph.D., "Stop the Escalator and Get Off," interview courtesy of Georgetown University Public Relations Department, Washington, D.C., May 1974.

Norman Mark, "Calm Down—At Your Own Risk," *Today's Health*, March 1974.

Jules H. Masserman, "The Neurotic Cat," *Psychology Today Reprint Series*, No. P–57 (October 1967), pp. 37–39, 56–57.

David Mechanic, "Discussion of Research Programs on Relations Between Stressful Life Events and Episodes of Physical Illness," *Stressful Life Events: Their Nature and Effects*, John Wiley & Sons, Inc., 1974, pp. 87–96.

Ms. Junx Melia, interview courtesy of Georgetown University Public Relations Department, Washington, D.C., 1974.

Neal E. Miller, "Learning of Visceral and Glandular Responses," *Science*, Vol. 163 (January 31, 1969).

Charles S. Mirabile, M.D., "Mental Illness and Susceptibility to Motion Sickness," *The American Journal of Psychiatry*, Vol. 128, No. 12 (June 1972), pp. 1550–1552.

Charles S. Mirabile, Jr., M.D., Bernard C. Glueck, M.D., and Charles F. Stroebel, Ph.D., M.D., "Spatial Orientation, Cognitive Process and Cerebral Specialization," Institute of Living, Hartford, Connecticut, March 1975, pp. 1–22.

Charles S. Mirabile, M.D., "Orienting Mechanisms and Behavior," *Psychiatric Annals,* 1973.

Dr. W. Hugh Missildine, Professor of Psychiatry, Ohio State University College of Medicine, interview with author, on tension, New York, January 1975.

"Neurosis, The Chronic Emergency," *Emergency Medicine* (February 1975), pp. 22–30.

Perry Nicassio and Richard Bootzin, "A Comparison of Progressive Relaxation and Autogenic Training as Treatments for Insomnia," *Journal of Abnormal Psychology,* Vol. 83, No. 3 (1974), pp. 253–260.

Dr. Irvine H. Page, "My Life and Hard Times in Hypertension," *Medical Tribune,* June 13, 1973, pp. 13–15.

Ferris N. Pitts, Jr., M.D., and James N. McClure, Jr., M.D., "Lactate Metabolism in Anxiety Neurosis," *New England Journal of Medicine,* 277(25), December 21, 1967, pp. 1329–1336.

Marjorie J. Raskin, "Biofeedback and Habituation Rates in Chronic Anxiety," *HEW Grant Abstract,* 1974.

Karl W. Rickels, M.D., "The Role of Tranquilizers in Medical Practice in the Control of Anxiety," A Symposium on Anxiety and a Decade of Tranquilizer Therapy, New York, April 1, 1964.

Eleanor B. Rodgerson, M.D., "Beyond the Menopause," *Geriatrics* (1972), pp. 30–31.

Arthur M. Sackler, M.D., A. Stanley Weltman, Ph.D., Vijay Pandhi, M.S., and L. Johnson, B.S., "Effects of Simulated-Subway Stress (SSS) on Reproductive and

Endocrine Function of Rats," 59th Annual Meeting of the Federation of American Societies for Experimental Biology, April 16, 1975.

Don A. Schanche, "Learn How a Psychologist Would Plan Your Vacation," *Today's Health,* June 1973, p. 54.

"Scientific Research on Transcendental Meditation," booklet from Maharishi International University, Los Angeles, California, 1972.

Julius Segal, Ph.D., "Biofeedback as a Medical Treatment," *The Journal of the American Medical Association,* Vol. 232, No. 2 (April 14, 1975).

Sydney J. Segal and Michael Glicksman, "Relaxation and the Perky Effect: The Influence of Body Position on Judgments of Imagery," *The American Journal of Psychology,* Vol. 80, No. 2 (June 1967), pp. 257–262.

Hans Selye, "The Concept of 'Stress'," *The Story of Psychosomatic Medicine* #2, Hoffmann-La Roche Inc., 1975.

Gary L. Singleton, M.D., "What Blaming Others Can Do to You," interview courtesy of Georgetown University Public Relations Department, Washington, D.C., 1974.

"Sleep-Inducing Factor May Lead to Insomnia Pill," *Modern Medicine,* March 1, 1975.

"Some Things You Should Know About Mental and Emotional Illness . . .," pamphlet from the National Association for Mental Health.

Donald P. Spence, Ph.D., "Human and Computer Attempts to Decode Symptom Language," *Psychosomatic*

Medicine, Vol. 32, No. 6 (November–December 1970), pp. 615–625.

George S. Stevenson, M.D., "How To Deal with Your Tensions," pamphlet from the National Association for Mental Health, 1957, pp. 3–15.

Eric A. Stone, "Neurochemical and Behavioral Effects of Severe Stress," *HEW Grant Abstract,* 1973.

Jerry M. Suls, Ph.D., "Humor Is Human," interview courtesy of Georgetown University Public Relations Department, Washington D.C., 1974.

"Ten Resolutions That Can Relieve Tensions," *Sunday Star-Ledger,* Newark, N.J., December 10, 1967.

Katherine Tennes, M.A., and Douglas Carter, M.D., "Plasma Cortisol Levels and Behavioral States in Early Infancy," *Psychosomatic Medicine,* Vol. 35, No. 2 (March–April 1973), pp. 121–128.

"Tension and Hypertension," *Patterns of Tension #3,* Hoffmann-La Roche Inc., 1975.

"Tensions of Advancing Age (II)," *Patterns of Tension #11,* Hoffmann-La Roche Inc., 1966.

Rev. John L. Thomas, S.J., "How To Do Nothing Better," interview courtesy of Georgetown University Public Relations Department, Washington, D.C., 1974.

Darold A. Treffert, M.D., "Oval Souls—Round Planets," personal communication with author, February 1975.

Paul L. Wachtel, Ph.D., "Wanting Nothing and Getting Nothing: On Negative Results in Hypnosis Research,"

The American Journal of Clinical Hypnosis, Vol. 11, No. 4 (April 1969) pp. 209–219.

Ingeborg L. Ward, "Prenatal Stress Feminizes and Demasculinizes the Behavior of Males," report, Villanova University, Villanova, Pa., 1973.

"What Makes Heart React to Emotion?" *The Journal of the American Medical Association,* Vol. 203, No. 5 (January 29, 1968), p. 33.

Ruth Winter, "A Few Somber Thoughts for a Gayer Vacation," *Sunday Star-Ledger,* Newark, N.J., April 3, 1966.

Ruth Winter, "Hormones for Depression," Los Angeles Times Syndicate, March 29–30, 1975.

Ruth Winter, "How to Make the Most of Your Time," Los Angeles Times Syndicate, August 1974.

Ruth Winter, "Is Vacation Needed After Your Vacation?" *Democrat and Chronicle,* Rochester, N.Y., June 22, 1974.

Ruth Winter, "Let Tots Slug It Out, M.D. Says; It's Healthy," Women's News Service, New York, October 24, 1962.

Ruth Winter, "Mind and Matter: Child's Tears Are Mental First Aid," Women's News Service, New York, January 8, 1965.

Ruth Winter, "Mind and Matter: Every Doctor Should Practice Psychiatry," Women's News Service, New York, January 29, 1965.

Ruth Winter, "Psychiatrist Says Tension May Benefit Some Persons," Women's News Service, New York, June 27, 1963.

Ruth Winter, "Psychologist Sees Guilt as Irrational Self-Hatred," Los Angeles Times Syndicate, April 14, 1974.

Ruth Winter, "The Mind Manipulators," Los Angeles Times Syndicate, January 1974.

Ruth Winter, "The Mind Manipulators: Chemical Manipulation of the Mind," Los Angeles Times Syndicate, January 1974.

Ruth Winter, "The Mind Manipulators: Manipulating Your Own Mind," Los Angeles Times Syndicate, January 1974.

Ruth Winter, "To Go or Not to Go to a Psychiatrist," Los Angeles Times Syndicate, March 1974.

Ruth Winter, "Uplifting Holiday Depression," Los Angeles Times Syndicate, December 15, 1974.

Ruth Winter, "What's So Funny?" Los Angeles Times Syndicate, January 1974.

Stewart Wolf and Harold G. Wolff, "Tom's Fistula—The Influence of Emotions on Gastric Function," *The Story of Psychosomatic Medicine #5*, Hoffmann-La Roche Inc., 1969, pp. 1–13.

D. W. Woolley, M.D., "Evidence to Support Relationship of Serotonin to Mental Diseases," *Roche Report: Frontiers of Clinical Psychiatry*, Vol. 3, No. 12 (June 15, 1966).

Richard J. Wurtman, M.D., "Control of Epinephrine Synthesis by the Pituitary and Adrenal Cortex: Possible Role in the Pathophysiology of Chronic Stress," *Recent Advances in Biological Psychiatry*, Vol. 9 (1967) pp. 359–368.

Index